# Car Free Cumbria

## Vol 1: North

First published in 2002 by John Gillham

British Library Cataloguing in Publication Data

A catalogue record of this book is available from the British Library.

ISBN 0 9540190-0-8

Printed by Carnmor Print and Design London Road, Preston

While every effort has been taken by the authors to ensure the accuracy of this book, changes do occur, and these may affect the contents. Neither the author nor the publisher accepts liability for these.

It is expected that walkers and climbers, or their companions, will be fully experienced in mountaincraft before setting out on the more serious expeditions.

# Car Free Cumbria

## Vol 1: North

**Walking the county using lake steamers, local buses and trains**

## By Jon Sparks

Editor: Ronald Turnbull

Maps and line drawings by John Gillham

John Gillham
Hoddlesden

Photos:
Front Cover: Walkers and launch at Barrow Bay, Derwent Water

**Check our web site at**

# www.johngillham.com

We intend posting online updates to all our books. If you know of routes or information that needs updating email us on info@johngillham.com

# Contents

Walk 1   Scafell Pike from sea-level:  Start: Ravenglass Finish: Dalegarth          11

Walk 2   Granite Delights:  Ravenglass to Dalegarth          16

Walk 3   Sail Beck and Newlands:  Buttermere to Keswick          21

Walk 4   Lorton and Ladyside:  Lorton to Braithwaite          24

Walk 5   Downhill Isn't Cheating:  Honister Pass to Derwentwater          28

Walk 6   Short but Sweet:  Lodore to Keswick          32

Walk 7   Beautiful Borrowdale to Derwentwater:  Seatoller to Keswick          36

Walk 8   Beyond the chocolate box:  Keswick to Watendlath and Rosthwaite          42

Walk 9   The not-so-ugly sister: a traverse of Skiddaw:  Bassenthwaite to Keswick   47

Walk 10  Lakeland's Only Lake:  Bassenthwaite to Keswick          52

Walk 11  The Best of Blencathra:  Mungrisedale to Keswick          56

Walk 12  The Noble Art of Bog-trotting:  Keswick to Ambleside          61

Walk 13  The Great Ridge:  Bridgend to Grasmere over The Dodds and Helvellyn  66

Walk 14  Above Ullswater:  Pooley Bridge to Glenridding          72

Walk 15  Top of the Pops:  Howtown to Glenridding          76

Walk 16  Not the Fairfield Horseshoe:  Patterdale to Ambleside          79

Sources of Information          85

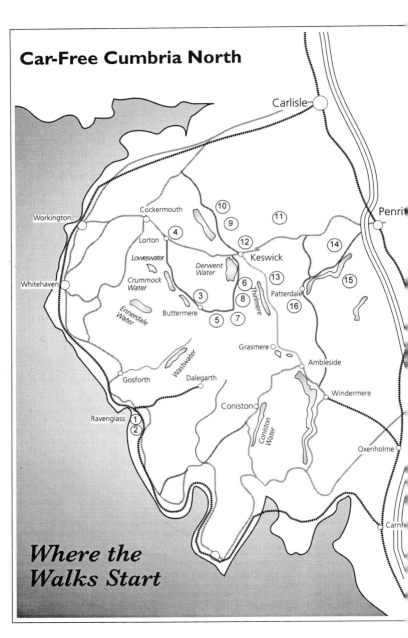

# Introduction

Walking is the most natural way of getting around, but there is nothing particularly natural about walking in circles. We are all descended from nomads, and walks that go from place to place appeal to something deep within us. Most of the great long walks, from the Pennine Way to the Appalachian Trail, are place-to-place walks. They are not just ways to get a bit of exercise amid some pleasant scenery; they are journeys. There is no reason why shorter walks should not share this sense of actually going somewhere.

And yet the overwhelming majority of guide books to the Lake District, and throughout Britain, are full of circular or, worse still, out-and-back walks. (We could call these 'closed' routes; place-to-place walks would then be 'open'.) There is a reason for this, but it's not a particularly good one. It is the assumption, usually unwritten and unquestioned, that every walk must start and finish at a parked car. Cars, to most people, represent mobility and freedom. Sometimes this is real, sometimes merely a seductive dream. It certainly has a hollow ring when you can't find a parking space in Borrowdale. Cars might be liberating as one option, but to see them as the only option is restricting.

Some guidebooks give the impression that there is no public transport in the Lake District. In fact the district is well covered, and in the last few years the level of service has actually been improving. One of the great pleasures of travelling around the Lakes is the sheer variety on offer: not just everyday trains and buses, but steam trains, open-top buses, lake cruises and the eccentric Windermere ferry. All of these allow you to look at something other than the car in front.

Let's face it, in a car, only the front-seat passenger can really enjoy the scenery. The driver ought to be looking at the road, and the back seats give a pretty restricted view. Even single-decker buses sit you higher than a car, with hitherto unsuspected views over walls and hedges. Trains and steamers give an entirely new perspective. The supreme example is the crossing of the River Kent on the Furness Line, where you can get whiplash from trying to look both ways at once. Scenically, it knocks the road route into a very small cocked hat.

So there are good selfish reasons to use public transport. You can feel good about it because of the environmental and social benefits. I hardly need to enumerate the environmental arguments; anyone who isn't familiar with them must have been living in a goldfish bowl for at least the last 10 years. On the social side, using local transport sustains jobs and helps to supports services on which many people still depend. However, the key point for us is that using public transport is the best and easiest way to enjoy a whole range of walks which simply aren't possible when you're tied to a car. There are many routes in the Lake District, whether crossing passes or following ridge systems, where an open walk is the natural choice. These are what this book is about.

A popular stratagem for some of the long ridges is to have two groups, a car at each end, and swap keys in the middle. Such arrangements are no use to solitary walkers, and aren't foolproof anyway. I was once in a group which set out to traverse the full High Street Ridge. Group A (including me) parked at Celleron, B at Troutbeck. We met and exchanged keys, as planned, on top of High Street. I left them with the parting words, 'just follow the Roman road'.

Group A was already back at base in Cockermouth and scoffing pizza when the phone rang. Group B's first words were, 'where the hell's your car?' Once I'd recovered, we established that they, using a different map, had followed a different Roman road and ended up in Bampton. It was already dark, Celleron is five miles from Bampton, and Bampton has a pub. Not surprisingly, Group B did not fancy finding the car for themselves. So someone (guess who?) had to drive out again from Cockermouth.

A walk from Celleron to Troutbeck can be arranged using public transport, but it isn't the most convenient, and so isn't in this book 2. This book concentrates on routes which are really easy to do with the help of public transport. This does include several classic ridge traverses, such as the Helvellyn range.

So how were the routes selected? I have assumed that walkers will not want to spend longer on the bus/boat/train than actually walking, so routes have been chosen to allow a reasonably convenient return to a starting point. This notional base town is for convenience only and it is not compulsory to use it! However, I have assumed that most people will either have a return ticket to a given centre, or accommodation there, or even (perish the thought!) a car parked there.

Some wonderfully attractive routes have been omitted because there is no simple way of linking the two end points. These would come into their own as part of a weekend or longer tour, but that will have to wait for another book. In general I have chosen routes which need only a single public transport stage to complete the day and return to base. There are a few minor exceptions, mostly where you can hop on one of the Derwentwater launches as an alternative to foot-slogging all the way back to Keswick.

The walks have been planned to avoid finishing in the middle of nowhere. All of them end up at towns or villages, or close to a pub or tea-shop. Finishing points have good transport links. Infrequent services are used, if at all, to get to the start.

This book is not for train-spotters. It is for walkers. The physical act of walking is the same whether you get to the start by car, bus or cycle rickshaw, but the shape and feel of the walk can be very different. Some of the walks in this book cover ground the circular walks miss. Others cover similar ground to well-known circular routes, but show it in a new light.

And when you look back on the day, there will be more to it than just another route ticked off: the smell of steam on the Ravenglass and Eskdale Railway, treetops parting your hair on a double-decker, the polished planking of the Derwentwater launches, the chance to sup a pint while Ullswater drifts past. Pity those whose day starts and finishes with the same old car every time.

## Using this book

It is not possible to give full timetables for all the services used for these walks. This would double the size of the book, and they would soon be out of date anyway. Rural bus services are currently increasing after years of decline, so many changes will be for the better. Full details are given of the route used, including bus service numbers, plus an indication of approximately when and how frequently the service runs, and where to join it. It would still be wise to check before setting out, especially where the journey depends on one of the more limited services.

The section on sources of information gives all the relevant addresses, phone numbers and - increasingly valuable - Internet addresses.

There are a few services aimed specifically at ramblers, but most bus and train services run throughout the year, and most of the walks in this book are feasible at any date. However, Sundays can be problematic. The Cumbrian Coast Line has no Sunday service at all, and other lines grind to a halt on Sunday mornings in winter. Bank Holidays (apart from Boxing Day and New Year) are also peculiar: most buses run to a Sunday timetable while train services retain the normal weekday pattern.

Each chapter has notes on the Character of the walk, and Distance and Time. Distance is (or at least should be!) the same for everyone but time will obviously vary. The suggested time allows for a reasonable pace and short stops for drinks and photography, but not extended breaks for meals or other diversions. Car connections are given in detail where required; usually all that is required is to find the main car park in the suggested local base town.

The description of the walk is intended to allow the walk to be followed with no further help. I still recommend that you carry the appropriate Ordnance Survey or Harvey's map, which will put the route in a wider context, as well as helping you to identify escape routes or other alternatives which are not described. Of course carrying the map is not enough: you also need to know how to use it. On one or two of the more remote walks, there are sections without paths, and if thick mist were to descend it would be important to know how to follow a compass bearing.

The final chapter, the Lakeland Skyline Walk, is a different kettle of fish, being an expedition which, for most people, will occupy five days. The description here is necessarily less detailed and it is essential to supplement it with maps.

### Where to catch your bus in Keswick.

In most places bus stops are obvious, and walk descriptions give further details. However, Keswick is the base for a large number of the walks. From the town centre (Moot Hall) walk west, through a short pedestrianised section, to a mini-roundabout. Turn left for 150m to the bus-station, beyond the Lakeland supermarket, which has a tea-room.

# Walk 1: Scafell Pike from Sea-level

*Ravenglass to Dalegarth*

| | |
|---|---|
| *Character:* | This is the longest day-walk in the book, and the toughest. There is a long gentle preamble before the real climbing starts at the head of Miterdale. The ground becomes very rough on Scafell Pike itself, and the crossing from the Pike to Scafell is rocky and spectacular. While there is no real scrambling involved, it could still be alarming for those of a nervous disposition. (Many guidebooks, including Wainwright, give details of the easier route via Foxes Tarn). |
| | Navigation can be difficult in misty conditions, both on the way off Scafell Pike and on the descent from Scafell, whose broad western slopes offer few landmarks. This final descent is not difficult but the last few kilometres are rough and tiring. These are the highest peaks in England and conditions on the tops usually bear little resemblance to those at sea level. |
| *Distance and Time:* | 29 km/ 18 miles, 1250m/ 4000 feet of ascent. Allow 11 hours |
| *Refreshments:* | Tea-rooms on both stations and pubs in Ravenglass and Boot. The Bower House Inn, Eskdale Green, is the only temptation during the walk itself. |
| *Local Base:* | Eskdale (Boot) or Ravenglass |
| *Local Transport:* | Ravenglass and Eskdale Railway. The timetable is complex, but there is good phone and on-line information. In summer the last train back from Eskdale is at 6 pm. If you are based in Eskdale the first train to Ravenglass is at 7.30 am on weekdays only, or at 10.10 am. Despite the fact that the terminus at Ravenglass is right alongside the Cumbrian Coast Line station, services are not exactly integrated. |

From sea-level to the highest point in England: who could resist? Probably anyone who doesn't like long walks. In which case it is worth

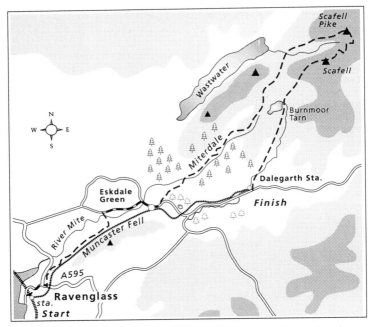

mentioning that one can start from Eskdale Green (Irton Road sta-tion). Such a truncated version of the walk misses out on a special kind of satisfaction, and on the rare sense of travelling on foot through a progression of environments, but still enjoys the unusual approach to Scafell Pike by Miterdale, a little-known but lovely valley.

Scafell Pike itself is hidden from view until you are almost upon its slopes. Arriving at its summit  may be a crowning moment, but the finest part of the walk is the crossing from here to Scafell.

Given the length of this walk, and the limited service on the Cumbrian Coast Line (none at all on Sundays), it is advisable to spend a night or even two in the area. Eskdale is probably the better bet, with pubs, B & B's and a campsite. One can then catch an early train down to Ravenglass and tackle the walk in relaxed fashion.

**THE WALK**: To do the job properly, you should start from sea-level, but this means that the first 200m are in precisely the wrong direction. From the platform at **Ravenglass**, walk past the turntable to the footbridge over the main line. Go down a footpath beside the car park and straight ahead to the main street.

If the tide is out, the walk could be significantly longer, but at least go down onto the shingle. Then head along the street out of the village, under both railway lines and up to the junction with the A595. Follow the pavement up the hill for 200m, then cross to a footpath running up and across the end of Muncaster Fell.

Keep straight on alongside a fence, ignoring a branch to the right near the crest of the ridge. When the path descends into woodland, fork right. The way rises gently for about half a kilometre. At a four-way junction take the path sharply back left, descending alongside a small beck, to emerge onto a broad track. Turn right, passing **Muncaster Mill**. This is a fascinating traditional water mill producing organic flour, but there's no time for sightseeing today. Continue along a forest track for over a kilometre until it draws close to the Ratty line again.

The next 300m, marked by white-topped posts, are rough and often wet. Cross the line and come out into fields. Keeping parallel to the track, then return to line-side. Continue past some sidings and then emerge into fields once more. Follow blue waymarks round the edge of the first field and go right, along a muddy track. Pass to the right of an old barn and in another 100m turn left onto a straight, solid track which runs up to Sandbank Farm.

Turn right along a quiet lane and follow it for almost 2km, finally climbing and then descending to a junction near the Bower House Inn. Follow the busier road past the inn and continue another 500m to a lane on the left. This looks private, with a gateway flanked by railings, but is a public road. Go down past the school, and in about a kilometre meet the River Mite. Where the tarmac peters out go left to a bridge and then bear right up the slope to join the farm track to Low Place.

Go right at the end of the farmyard, with a bridleway sign. Notice, but don't follow, the dialect instructions on a board set in the wall just round the corner. Stay on this side of the river to follow a broad but rough path for another kilometre to Bakerstead, an outdoor centre for Egremont's Wyndham School. Cross a footbridge beside the house then bear left between ruins to climb a steep grassy corridor between forestry plantations. Watch out for red squirrels in this area.

The slope eases as the corridor broadens; keep right of centre on a vague path connecting the gates through several enclosures. At a final gate onto open moorland the path ahead is clear enough, still rising

**The Way up Scafell Crag**

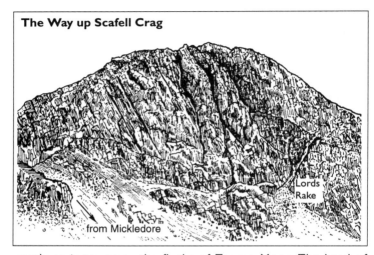

Lords Rake

from Mickledore

gently as it traverses the flanks of Tongue Moor. The head of **Miterdale**, down to the right, grows steeper and more enclosed, becoming a private little valley which was probably one model for Arthur Ransome's Swallowdale.

As the way swings round more to the north, Burnmoor Tarn lies below, while ahead a broad saddle appears. Kirk Fell rises directly behind, with Great Gable appearing over the side of Scafell. A beeline to the saddle seems tempting but crosses wet ground; the path rises gradually before joining the more trodden way down from Illgill Head to the saddle.

From the saddle the main path descends towards Wasdale Head. To avoid any loss of height, bear away to its right and contour round the hillside, crossing Groove Gill and Hollow Gill. There's no real path, just sporadic sheep-trods. The wall on the left climbs gradually towards us and we meet it at its highest point, below the broken Rakehead Crag.

Scafell Pike is now seen for the first time, still high above on the right. Continue gently rising across the rough fellside. Brown Tongue lies ahead, with becks either side and an obvious path on its crest. Aim for a substantial cairn where its slope eases below the bouldery combe of **Hollow Stones**. Fork left here on a clear path, below the west-facing Pikes Crag, to the Lingmell col. Swing back right to climb **Scafell Pike's** final stony slopes to the huge cairn at the roof of

England. (That's what almost everyone calls it, but if it's a roof why doesn't it keep the rain off?)

From the summit head southwest over boulder-strewn slopes. A little grass is seen as the way descends to the col of **Mickledore**. Scafell Crag is right in front all the way, with the barrel-shaped East Buttress round to the left. The main crag has climbs of all grades, but the steeper East Buttress offers no scope for easier climbing.

At Mickledore there is an awkward choice. The shortest way to Scafell is dead ahead, by Broad Stand, the obvious weakness between Scafell Crag and the East Buttress. However there is an exposed and very awkward scramble at the start, which has claimed several lives. This is for experienced scramblers only.

Instead descend scree to the right and follow a narrow path along the base of Scafell Crag, (There is a higher but more awkward alternative, known as Rake's Progress, which starts by scrambling up and right from the end of Mickledore).

The Central Buttress of Scafell is the most famous rock-climb in the Lakes. The crucial pitch, the overhanging Flake Crack, is prominent in the centre of the wall. Always hard, this became a good deal harder a few years ago when the crucial chockstone, which had supported thousands of climbers, came away. The climber was killed.

After Central Buttress pass below two obvious gullies, Moss Gill and Steep Gill, and along the base of Scafell Pinnacle, before climbing ahead up an obvious stone-filled slanting break. This is **Lord's Rake**. Just before the col at the top of the first section go left along a once-grassy shelf with a well-worn path, the West Wall Traverse. This leads into the upper section of Deep Gill. Take care, and try not to dislodge stones as the lower part of the Gill is very steep, and there could be climbers or walkers passing beneath.

Emergence is fairly sudden, with the top of Scafell Pinnacle on the left. The summit of **Scafell** itself is still a good 300m away across easy stony slopes.

Descend to the west. The main path heads down towards Wasdale, while the leftward branch is indistinct and easily missed, but it hardly matters. About a kilometre from the summit, on **Green How**, the slope eases noticeably. Turn south-west down a vague ridge, Hard Rigg. The path is clearer lower down where it cuts a grassy line through the bracken. As the way levels out, head across boggy ground to a footbridge at the outlet of **Burnmoor Tarn**.

Turn left on a clear track, a former corpse road, rising gently over Eskdale Moor. Now very rough in places, it must have been better maintained when bodies were regularly carried from Wasdale to Eskdale for burial in consecrated ground. Follow it across the open moor for about two kilometres, the first slightly rising, the second descending.

The descent gets a little steeper at the first gate, and it is still more than a kilometre through the enclosures to the final twist down to the bridge at the end of **Boot** village. If you have a train to catch, bear in mind it is still ten minutes walk to **Dalegarth** station.

# Walk 2: Granite Delights

*Ravenglass to Dalegarth*

| | |
|---|---|
| *Character:* | Good paths and tracks, plus a few short stretches of road. Muncaster Fell can be wet underfoot after heavy rain. Navigation is straightforward. |
| *Distance and Time:* | 15 km/ 9 miles, 300m/ 1000 feet of ascent. Allow 5¹/₂hrs |
| *Refreshments:* | There are tea-rooms at both ends of the Ratty, plus the Ratty Arms on the main-line platform at Ravenglass and several pubs in or near Boot. The King George IV Inn at Eskdale Green is handily placed in the middle of the walk. |
| *Local Base:* | Eskdale (Boot) or Ravenglass |
| *Local Transport:* | Ravenglass and Eskdale Railway. The timetable is complex, but in summer the last train back from Eskdale is at 6pm. The first trains from Eskdale to Ravenglass are at 7.30 am on weekdays, 10.10 am on weekends. |
| | Although the terminus at Ravenglass is right alongside the Cumbrian Coast Line station, R and E R literature seems to assume visitors will come by car, and timetables are not integrated. (On the other hand the splendid Ratty Arms is right on the platform - that's my idea of integrated transport!) This walk can be done from Lancaster or Carlisle in a day, but not on Sundays. |

Whilst not the only walk in this book from sea-level to the heart of Lakeland, this it is certainly the easiest. Ravenglass, the estuary, Roman remains and the sylvan grounds of Muncaster Castle fill the early stages with incident. Stretch the legs and drink in the views over

Muncaster Fell, which provides the meat of the walk, then finish along the dale, with a final side-jaunt to the exotic Stanley Force.

In combination with a ride on La'al Ratty, as the Ravenglass and Eskdale Railway is properly known, this is a quintessential Lakeland day out.

*The Ravenglass and Eskdale Railway near Eskdale Green*

**THE WALK:** Once the Ratty has whisked you in air-conditioned comfort down to **Ravenglass**, walk past the turntable to a footbridge over the main line. Go down a footpath by the car park and straight ahead to the main street. Go left to its end, where the estuary opens up, backed by sand-hills and the distant bulk of Black Combe. If the tide is very high it may be necessary to back-track (recross the footbridge and continue 150m to a lane then turn right to Walls Castle). Normally, follow the shoreline left for 200m then go up a short track and a footpath to the left of a gate. Go under the main line (headroom about 180cm) then fork right to a tarmac lane. Go right along this, passing **Walls Castle**. This is the remains of a Roman bath-house and has some of the tallest Roman masonry in the country.

Two hundred metres further on take a stony track to the left, climbing gently to Newtown. The tiny chapel incorporated into the farm buildings is worth a glance. Almost opposite, a footpath sign

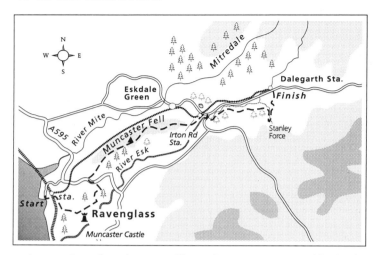

points up through a plantation. The path is sometimes muddy. At the top go over a stile into a field and bear slightly left, still rising gently. Keep to the left of the highest ground. A wall ahead encloses a wood: to the right of its highest point are a stile and gate.

Go gently downhill on a clear path with yellow-topped guideposts, through the grounds of **Muncaster Castle**. The walk gives a free taste of the delights available to paying customers, notably the famous rhododendrons. Descend more steeply, cross the lawn and pass just left of the Stable Yard. The track curves left past the church then straight up to the main road.

Go left, on a good footway, for 350m to a sharp bend. Go right on a stony track (Fell Lane) and climb steadily for almost a kilometre. The track dips slightly and then forks. Go right here, then left at another fork 100m further on, to resume the ascent through rhododendrons. Muncaster Tarn is just glimpsed on the left. After a gate the track becomes more level, with the summit of the fell appearing ahead. The distant pointed peak to its right is Bowfell. The path, rougher now, runs alongside a plantation. At its end keep left for a few metres then head directly across open slopes of bracken and scattered gorse to the **Muncaster Fell's** summit trig point.

358 degrees of the view will delight almost everyone. Scafell (hiding Scafell Pike), Bowfell and Crinkle Crags rise at the head of the valley.

Your response to the remaining 2 degrees will depend on your feelings about nuclear power.

Drop steeply east between rocky humps to level ground and after 30m find a narrower path to the right, skirting the southern side of Hooker Moss past some sculpted granite outcrops. Dodge another wet patch before things settle down. Upright stones line the path and then there is a stone table with the inscription **Ross's Camp** 1883, built as a luncheon spot for shooting parties. From here the path swings left and down then across more wet stuff to a gap in a wall. The valley of Miterdale lies dead ahead, pointing to Scafell.

The next descent is often wet. Splash down to a broad saddle with scattered birch and rowan and the odd rhododendron. Cross this to an obvious built-up track rising round the right side of a knoll and a final, drier, descent towards the green fields of upper Eskdale. At the bottom go through a gate in a wall, wind through the gorse of Rabbit How and down a bit more to a transverse track.

Go right a few metres to a gate and stile then immediately left across the field, past a prominent boulder, towards the corner of a wall enclosing a plantation. The ground can be churned by cattle but is generally best close to the wall. Keep this on your left through the next field then go down, under trees again, to an enclosed ford with stepping stones. After a stile the path bears left between walls. Join a tidy track (**Eskdale Green** station is just above), and go right to a road then right again for 300m to the King George IV inn.

Go down the road on the right for another 300m. Cross Forge Bridge then take a bridleway on the left alongside the Esk. Pass the cottage of Milkingstead, then a large shed and a footbridge on the left. 300m further on, the track swings away from the river. Go over a stile by the right hand gate then along the left edge of a field. A cobbled path past a ruin leads back towards the river.

After a pleasant section through birch woods and a slight climb with some smooth bare rock, the track runs into **Low Wood**, losing touch with the river. Keep on for nearly a kilometre through very mixed woodland, with some tall cypress among the more usual suspects.

At the top of a slight rise the track forks: keep right, peeking over the wall at lovely Dalegarth Hall. 250m beyond this go right on a clearer track signed to Stanley Gill, Birker Fell, then straight ahead through a gate marked Waterfalls, entering a National Park Access Area.

Follow the track round right and up alongside the gill, crossing and recrossing via three footbridges. The valley becomes a shady gorge, its rocky walls smothered in lush greenery. Rhododendrons add a

Himalayan touch; in fact the whole ambience is exotic. However, rhododendrons are bad for biodiversity as they squeeze out most other species. Valiant efforts are being made to contain them but it looks, all too literally, an uphill task.

Take note of the warning on the third bridge. There should be an earlier warning about the dangers of tripping over warning signs. Don't go (too far) past the next notice. Deeply enclosed, **the Force** itself is more powerful than beautiful. From the third bridge another path climbs to a further viewpoint at the brink of a granite crag, but this is optional. Retrace and follow the gill all the way down to cross a fourth footbridge.

Go straight ahead from the gate on a green path dividing bracken to meet the Esk again then go upstream for 100m to stepping stones. If the river is abnormally high and these are awash, it's tempting to wade alongside, but the water will then be knee-deep on a person who is 179 cm tall (I take my research seriously). In this case the sensible thing to do is to backtrack past the last footbridge then bear right on a permitted path to a parking area and out on a track to the valley road 300m west of **Dalegarth** station.

In normal conditions, cross to St Catherine's Church, then go down the track past the church gate and out via Esk View Farm to the road. The side-road to Boot is immediately opposite, beside the Brook House Inn, while Dalegarth station is 250m along the road to the left.

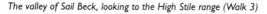

*The valley of Sail Beck, looking to the High Stile range (Walk 3)*

# Walk 3: Sail Beck and Newlands

*Buttermere to Keswick*

| | |
|---|---|
| Character: | A steady climb on a clear path, followed by a steeper descent with some loose sections. The later stages are a mix of lanes, tracks and field paths. It would be hard to get lost. |
| Distance and Time: | 14 km/ 9 miles, 400m/ 1300 feet of ascent. Allow 5 1/2 hours. By catching the Derwentwater Launch from Hawse End, you can cut 4 km from the end of the walk. |
| Refreshments: | Pubs and tearooms in Buttermere. Cafe at Nichol End Marina and pubs in Portinscale. |
| Local Base: | Keswick |
| Local Transport: | The Honister Rambler Buses 77 and 77A each make four departures daily from Keswick, from the beginning of May to the end of October. The clockwise 77A is slightly quicker to Buttermere than the anti-clockwise 77. |

There are many well-trodden routes over the hills between Buttermere and Keswick but this is a way through them, using the deep, symmetrical valleys of Sail Beck and Rigg Beck. In this case, at least, valley walking is both quieter and easier than ridge-walking and one is never totally hemmed in. Finally a short crossing of pastoral Newlands leads to the shores of Derwentwater and a level (and optional) finish into Keswick.

**The Walk:** The bus stops behind the Bridge hotel in Buttermere village. Walk out to the main road, go left over the bridge and then up a footpath on the right alongside Mill Beck. After 400m climb away from the beck and then go right, just above a wall. Keep to the lowest path, looking back for views over the lake to the High Stile range.

The path develops into a good, gently rising, grassy track, which keeps almost parallel to the Newlands road across the valley. The road pulls away above the confluence of a side stream (Swinside Gill), also marked by a substantial sheepfold. Opposite this point, our path forks: take the stonier left branch, climbing steadily for five minutes to join another level path. Swing left into the little side valley between

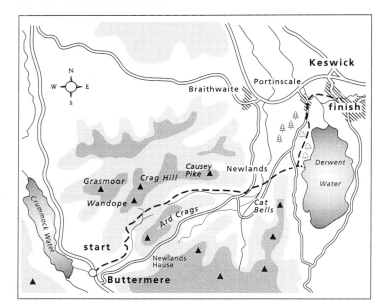

Whiteless Breast and Bleak Rigg and go up until the path slides down to the beck. Cross, and ascend a green track through bracken. Where the gradient eases, look across right to Newlands Hause and the waterfall just above. Ahead, not quite on the skyline, is the col which is the high point of the route.

The path swings into a second side valley, confusingly called **Third Gill**. Climb alongside the beck for a few minutes before crossing it to the start of a fine, long, almost level traverse of an even grassy slope. The knobbly outline of Causey Pike looms over the col, while a glance back reveals High Stile and High Crag. Red Pike appears later to complete the triptych.

A third side valley (Addacomb Beck) signals the start of the final climb to the col, initially over scree. This is multicoloured, averaging out to a pinkish hue. Where heather is met, the path forks. Keep right, running low and almost level to the col. Look back before leaving the valley of **Sail Beck**. This shows not a glaciated 'U' shape but the 'V' of a river-carved valley. When the light is right (mid-afternoon) the pattern of interlocking spurs in the upper valley is very striking.

At the col, the view opens ahead. Clough Head appears first, then Stybarrow Dodd. The path winds in slow descent across heathery slopes. Before much height is lost the path forks: take the lower right branch, which becomes quite steep, with sections of shifting stones. The surroundings are heather, with accents of bilberry and a little bracken. The loose ground demands attention, so the unfolding of the view seems to happen almost by stealth. A pause in the downward career allows the whole Helvellyn ridge to be seen.

A stony traverse runs below a stand of oaks. Like the better-known oaks at Keskadale, on the other side of the Ard Crags ridge, these may be remnants of the woodland which once covered the fells. The valleys were cleared with axes, first stone, later iron, while on the higher ground sheep have done most of the damage. Parsley-fern abounds here. The resemblance to the herb is obvious but coincidental: ferns are an entirely different order of plants.

A gentler descent follows before the final dip, meeting the road at a small bridge just below a purple house. Go left for about 600m to a wooden gate on the right with a footpath sign (Ghyll Brow 1/2 mile). Go down to a drive, straight across and down fields, with some wet bits, to a footbridge over Newlands Beck. Up on the other side by a second footbridge to the lane by **Ghyll Bank** farm. Go left 50m to a footpath on the right (Skelghyll), then over a stile by an iron gate and on in the same line through a field.

Cross another stile by a triple-trunked ash tree then follow field edges to Skelghyll. Keep right of the first house and go up the track to a lane, met on a bend. Go up right, and through a gate. Now the lane tips down again, with Skiddaw and Blencathra seen ahead. Join a wider road at a hairpin bend at the foot of Catbells. Descend over a cattle grid to a footpath on the right at a second hairpin.

Follow this down to a crossroads, and a choice: go right 50m then left to get the boat back; turn half left on the footpath to continue to Keswick. This takes a fairly direct and always clear line through woodland and fields. At a white house, the lodge to the grand Lingholm, go through a gate and continue on a clear broad track signed for Keswick. A fine set of chimneys is seen on the right, then another house ahead. Just left of this a short footpath goes down to Nichol End landings, offering a cafe and a final chance to finish by boat.

Go left on the access track to the road and turn right. Go past a marina and into **Portinscale**. Just past the Village Store the main road swings left while we go right, passing the Derwentwater Hotel. Cross a bouncing bridge into a quiet road. After 200m a track goes right through fields. At its end go left alongside the river to the main road then turn right into town.

## Walk 4: Lorton and Ladyside

*Lorton to Braithwaite (optional continuation to Keswick)*

| | |
|---|---|
| Character: | A simple division of ascent into distance shows that this is the steepest walk in this book. Most of the ascent is concentrated into a very steep climb onto the Ladyside Pike ridge, while the descent of Grisedale Pike falls into three sharp stages. In between there is plenty of relatively gentle ridge-walking. The first half is generally grassy, with stony paths later, eroded in places coming off Grisedale Pike. There is a short easy scramble onto Hobcarton Crag. Navigation should pose no problems. The extension from Braithwaite to Keswick is mostly on tarmac. |
| Distance and Time: | 11 km/ 7 miles, 900m/ 2950 feet of ascent. Allow 6 hours. Continuing to Keswick adds 5$^1$/2 km but is virtually flat. |
| Refreshments.: | Braithwaite has several pubs, notably the Coledale Inn, and there is a cafe on the camping/caravan site. |
| Local Base: | Braithwaite or Keswick |
| Local Transport: | From the beginning of May to the end of October, the Honister Rambler Bus 77 makes four departures daily from Keswick, passing through Braithwaite a few minutes later. Ask to be let off at High Lorton. The counter-service 77A may be useful for a return to Keswick from Braithwaite. The X5 Penrith to Workington service provides useful connections for those based in Braithwaite. Outside the summer season, the walk can be done using X5 to Cockermouth and service 265 (Fridays only) or dial-a-ride service 949 (Monday to Saturday) from there to Lorton. |

Elegant Grisedale Pike is one of the most attractive peaks in view from the Keswick area. Car-bound walkers generally tackle it either as a straight up-and-down or as part of the Coledale Horseshoe. The liberated walker can choose from several attractive alternatives. A straight ridge-walk from Crummock Water via Whiteside is appealing, but our route wins on two counts: its delightful approach from Lorton and the little-frequented ridge of Ladyside Pike. This has an exciting finish with easy scrambling and fine views of Hobcarton Crag.

**The Walk**: From the big bend in the road in **Lorton** go up a narrow lane signposted Boon Beck and Scales. After 300m take a footpath on the right to Scales. Go through a metal gate by a barn then in front of a house and up a track. 10m past a bend a footpath sign points to the right up a stony track. This rises steadily, becoming grassier after it bends right. Climb gently for almost 1km to High Swinside Farm, enjoying widening views over the Vale of Lorton. This is a lovely appetiser, of a kind that the car-bound walker usually misses. At **High Swinside** go through a wooden gate then to the left of the farm buildings. Cross a cattle grid and go straight up to a narrow lane.

   Almost opposite, a green track rises to the right up the steep hillside. Follow this and then break back left, rising to a gate in a wall. Pick the best line, before or alongside the wall, up the steep slope. In summer the main criterion is avoiding the bracken. Whichever line you pick, the slope is very steep, zig-zags are essential and the calf muscles will certainly protest. Fortunately there's only about 100m to climb before the slope begins to ease.

   Bear right along the crest of the ridge, following an old wall. Bracken gives way to heather and then to pale grass. The increasingly ruinous wall, supplemented by a wire fence, is a clear guide.

   As the ridge levels off it becomes easier to look around. Grisedale Pike, Ladyside Pike and Hopegill Head appear in front, with Skiddaw and Blencathra away to the left. Behind, the Vale stretches towards Cockermouth and in the distance are the Solway Firth and the hills of Galloway.

   The ridge kinks left, dipping slightly, before the final rise onto Ladyside Pike, with the old wall still struggling alongside. Look down into the depths of Hope Gill and be glad I didn't send you that way. It's marked as a right of way but there's no obvious path, while the climb out is just as steep as our climb onto the ridge and a lot longer.

   A large cairn stands just before the highest point. At the summit cross to the left of the wall for a slight descent to a col. A stepped ridge now rears ahead. The path avoids the first step but it can be tackled head on, though you may need to take your hands out of your pockets.

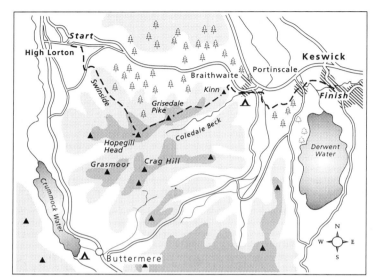

A grassy crest and rocky platforms before the second step make a great lunch spot, with views down and across the sagging wreckage of Hobcarton Crag. This clearly is not a crag to draw climbers or scramblers, but is of rich botanical interest, notably as the only English site for the Alpine Catchfly (Viscaria alpina).

Again the path slinks right at the second step but again, if you approach direct, it lies back, though it falls short of rolling over to have its tummy tickled. In dry conditions the climb is easy enough, though the Skiddaw Slate is shattered and unreliable, and when wet is slippery too. Splendidly, the top of the step is the summit of **Hopegill Head**.

Fifty metres down to the left the path forks: keep to the left along the brink of Hobcarton Crag. The main path keeps a discreet distance from the crumbling edges. At the lowest point a (relatively) solid platform looks down the central gully and back across the crag.

Rising again, the path acquires another old wall for company. A slight rise gives the first sight of Keswick, Derwentwater, and the deep trough of Coledale. A broad highway now climbs steadily to **Grisedale Pike**. The rocky top has a modest cairn and far from modest view.

Continue in the same direction. If it happens to be misty, just be sure not to get on to the path which follows a ruined wall down to

Whinlatter. The Braithwaite path swings a little right from the angle of the wall then heads straight down, almost due east. It is steep and eroded as it descends about 150m, running out onto the easier ridge of Sleet How. From this you can look down over the sinuous course of Coledale Beck and up to the valley head, where Force Crag rises above the rusting remains of a barytes mine.

This interlude is followed by another chunk of descent, slanting down right to the broader brackeny ridge of **Kinn**. This teases with a slight rise before the final stage of the descent. The path drops down alongside a plantation, mostly larch, then swings left over a stile by a clump of trees. The map shows a right of way diving straight at the roofs of **Braithwaite** but this would be insanely steep.

The true path descends sensibly, with a view of Bassenthwaite Lake, then sweeps back right, traversing a steep slope above the Whinlatter road. Descend steps to a parking area and then follow the road to the village, finishing alongside the beck. By the 30 sign the lane to the Coledale Inn goes off right, while 50m straight ahead is another lane. Go down here past Ivy House Hotel and turn right, then first left. The bus stop is 150m away.

If you want to walk back to Keswick, which might unravel the legs after the steep descent, there is a footpath on the right 100m before the bus stop. This follows the beck, skirting a sizable caravan site. Escape into a field then cross a footbridge to a track, following the beck but now on the right bank, until it meets Newlands Beck. Follow this upstream to Little Braithwaite Farm. A permitted path avoids the farmyard and leads quickly to a lane.

Go down left and over a bridge with a view up Newlands to Catbells, Maiden Moor and Dale Head. At the next junction go left (Ullock) under the steep slopes of Swinside. This narrow lane is part of the C2C cycle route. Ullock is one large farm with two fine old barns and several sprawling modern sheds. Just past Yew Tree Cottage, a footpath on the left joins a muddy farm track. A surfaced path continues across further fields.

Cross a footbridge and climb slightly between beech hedges into **Portinscale**. At a tarmac lane go left 10m then right on a path which becomes a track, in suburban surroundings. At the road go right 100m then left up a lane with a footpath sign. At a left-hand bend take the lane on the right. As this too swings left keep straight on over a stile and down to the River Derwent.

Go right, upstream, for about 150m. Things feel rural again, but only briefly. Cross a bouncing bridge to a quiet road. After 200m a

*On the ridge between Hopegill Head and Grisedale Pike*

track goes right through fields. At its end go left on a lane by the river to the main road then right into town.

## Walk 5: Downhill Isn't Cheating

*Honister Pass to Derwentwater*

This walk starts 250m higher than it finishes. Some people may call it cheating, but this is sour grapes. Perhaps we should start all our walks from sea level (in which case the first ascent of Everest was made by Tim McCartney Snape). Perhaps we should all be entirely self-propelled from the moment we leave home (in which case the first ascent of Everest was made by Tensing, but not by Hillary).

Why not save all the arguments for the pub and just enjoy this walk? The High Spy - Catbells - Maiden Moor ridge is deservedly popular and this is the easiest way to do it. Not cheating, just great value. **The Walk:** The bus stops by **Honister Youth Hostel**, which is

| | |
|---|---|
| *Character:* | Mostly straightforward walking on well-defined tracks, stony in places. A few stretches of fairly steep descent can be slippery. Navigation is simple, apart from the short link from Yewcrag Quarries to Dalehead Tarn, which might require a little thought in poor visibility. |
| *Distance and Time:* | 9 km/ 6 miles, 470m/ 1550 feet of ascent (though downhill overall). |
| *Refreshments:* | Nothing en route |
| *Local Base:* | Keswick. Borrowdale would also be convenient, or of course the Honister Youth Hostel. |
| *Local Transport:* | The Honister Rambler Bus 77A has four departures daily from the beginning of May to the end of October. This is a circular route and the clockwise 77A gives a shorter approach to Honister than its anti-clockwise counterpart, 77. |
| | Derwentwater launches provide an easy return to Keswick. Again the clockwise service is preferable. Alternatively, a short hop on the anti-clockwise boat to Lodore allows you to finish by Walk 6 (Lodore to Keswick). Services are roughly hourly and continue until after 8 pm. To finish all the way into Keswick on foot see Walk 4 |

near enough to the top of the pass. Crossing the road gives five level metres of warm-up before tackling the slope of Dale Head, on green tracks through the bracken. These angle leftward towards a fence; there is no real need to cross this, except to get the best views down the far side of the pass. These are well displayed from about 100m above the youth hostel. The Buttermere valley plays second fiddle to the vast expanse of Honister Crag, scarred by old quarry workings and inclines.

A good place to re-cross the fence is at a steepening decked with slabby rocks, another 50m higher. The main path on the right of the fence is particularly stony hereabouts, but soon eases and becomes grassy again as it angles away from the fence. Break off to the right here, just below some heaps of quarry spoil (Yewcrag Quarries),

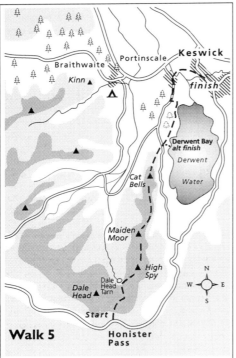

Walk 5

following a faint track along a slight shelf, which rises much more gently.

In short order you find yourself over-looking a broad marshy plateau with some small pools. Slant down left into an ill-defined valley, actually the upper reaches of Newlands Beck. The ground is drier if you keep to the left of the stream and aim for **Dale Head Tarn**, which sits on a shelf just above the beck. The main track from Dale Head to High Spy crosses below the tarn, near where the beck starts to dive into Newlands.

Ahead now is a clear stony track which climbs a short way right of Miners' Crag.

Although Newlands has a long history of mining, principally for lead, the miners in question are probably a group of men from the west Cumbrian coal pits, led by Bill Peascod, who pioneered the rock-climbs here in the 1940s. Peascod worked his way up from the coal face to become a mining engineer and later emigrated to Australia and forged a new life as an artist. In the 1980s he returned to Cumbria and to Lakeland climbing, and was seen by millions standing on Chris Bonington's shoulders in a TV film.

The summit of **High Spy** has one of the finest cairns in the district, along with views to justify the name, though broad eastern flanks obscure most of Borrowdale. Bassenthwaite is the only lake in sight but then, as any pedant will tell you, Bassenthwaite is the only lake in the Lake District.

Leaving the summit, keep left at the first dip and rise. Anyone with a half-decent head for heights should venture out along the rocky promontories which peer down the gullies of Eel Crag. These frame a superb picture across the head of Newlands to the dark north face of Dale Head and the elegant ridge of Hindscarth.

Five hundred metres further on, a rocky rise on the right, above Blea Crag, is worth visiting for its almost complete view of Derwentwater. Immediately after this comes the sharper drop-off to the ridge of Narrow Moor. This is one of those names you simply can't argue with. The next kilometre, as the ridge broadens out again, gives the easiest walking on the route. Indeed Maiden Moor is one of those rare summits which is reached by walking downhill. (This apparent paradox makes perfect sense on the ground).

The path swings east then gradually sweeps back northward again on an easy downward slope. All this grassy ambling is too good to last, and the final descent to Hause Gate is steep and eroded in places. Care is advisable, especially if the slaty rocks are wet. Erosion is inescapable on the rise to **Catbells**, one of the most popular fells in Lakeland. Surprisingly, however, its bare summit has no real cairn.

One has to ask what makes Catbells such a favourite. Perhaps the whimsical name gives it a head start. (How many devotees know that it is really Cat Bields, the lair of the wild cat?) Its modest height is presumably an attraction too, though its steepness makes you work for the altitude. That all-round steepness also makes it a grand viewpoint, with depth as well as distance on all sides. Derwentwater and Skiddaw are the stars of the panorama, though most people are here when the light is poor for photographing them.

The descent is in two, distinctly steep, stages, with a level intermission. Slivers of slate make some stretches of the descent quite musical. Wooden barriers have been emplaced to steer you onto the zigzags. Please respect these as any attempts at short-cuts will make the erosion worse. Near the bottom the path forks: go right here then left on reaching the road.

A path on the right cuts off the hairpin bend above the cattle-grid. Just below this take the track on the right, down to another lane. If you want to walk all the way back to Keswick, go left here and pick up the description in Walk 4. Otherwise, go right for 50m to a footpath on the left with a sign for Launch Jetty. Stroll the last 250m through the woods to the shore: frenzied sprints are only necessary if the

*Maiden Moor seen across Derwentwater. The walk is on the skyline.*

launch is already approaching.
Downhill? Cheating? Tell that to the skiing fraternity.

## Walk 6: Short but Sweet

*Lodore to Keswick*

Alert readers will have noticed the possibility of adding this walk as an extension to Walk 7 (Honister to Derwentwater). It's certainly a great way to round off the day, and the level walking should relax legs battered by rougher stuff. However, don't dismiss this as a mere appendix. Derwentwater is a beautiful lake and this walk follows nearly all of its eastern shore. It will hardly stretch to a full day, unless you are seriously into paddling and picnicking, but for an evening  or short day it's perfect, not least because it catches the afternoon sun.

| | |
|---|---|
| *Character:* | The shortest, flattest and therefore the easiest walk in this book. There is scarcely any ascent, unless you choose to make a closer inspection of Lodore falls, and uneven ground is only encountered in these early stages. Most of the terrain is easier than some city pavements. As for navigation, if you get lost on this let me know and I'll send you a medal. |
| *Distance and Time:* | 6 km/ 4 miles, 40m/ 130 feet of ascent. Allow 2 hours, but take as long as you feel like. |
| *Refreshments:* | Possibilities at Lodore, and again near the landing stages on the way back into Keswick. |
| *Local Base:* | Keswick |
| *Local Transport:* | Derwentwater Launch to Lodore. This service runs regularly in summer but at weekends only in winter. The clockwise service is more direct, though that isn't necessarily an advantage. |

**The Walk:** From the landing stage walk up to the road, then right, past the Lodore hotel to a drive on the left signed to The Falls. Follow signs behind the hotel buildings, passing an honesty box. The requested fee is 20p. I'm sure it was sixpence when I was a kid (I may be giving away my age here), and that can't possibly have kept pace with inflation.

Cross an iron bridge and go up right 100m to view the famous **Lodore Falls.** Worth 20p? Your reaction may depend on the amount of water coming down. The view is better in winter, when there's usually more water and less obscuring foliage. If you fancy exploring further, a steep path climbs to the left of the falls, or you can scramble over and around boulders (often greasy) to the foot of the cascades.

This is not the most impressive fall in the Lake District, but it is probably the best of the easily accessible ones. Its reputation hangs on Robert Southey's exuberant 'The Cataract of Lodore', which obviously describes the falls in spate. The whole thing reads like a thesaurus of wild wet words:

'...Flying and flinging,
Writhing and ringing,
Eddying and whisking,
Spouting and frisking...'

and so on. There are 151 'ands'.

Return to the guide-post and bear right on a clear path which returns

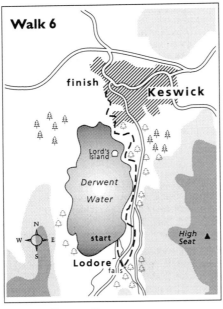

towards the road. A permissive path runs through the woods roughly parallel to the road, crossing **Cat Gill** on a footbridge. Just after this return to the road and cross it, skirting the corner of a car-park among trees to follow the lake shore on a convenient concrete shelf just below the road.

After 300m both shore and path swing away from the road. The next stretch is a delight, with good turf underfoot and great views. At a wooden footbridge the ground changes to shingle. Falcon Crags, Upper and Lower, rise ahead as the direction swings to the east into Barrow Bay.

The Lower Crag is popular with climbers, and brightly clad figures may well be seen on any dry day. The Upper Crag, which has some loose rock, is usually deserted, though one celebrated hard route crosses the smooth wall high on the left. The crown of the crag is a superb viewpoint, visited by Walk 9.

The next stile leads back to the road, with a bus stop just above and a landing stage 300m on, though surely these are only of academic interest. Continue along the shore, over and round trees and then round some steep rocks on a little 'causeway' just before the shore leaves the road. This can be awash if the lake is very high, in which case a short detour by the road avoids the obstacle.

An obvious made path now bisects the angle between road and shore. This is a permissive path, but there seems to be no objection to following the shore if you prefer. A footbridge crosses a small beck. Unless the Ordnance Survey have made a rare error, this is a second **Cat Gill** less than 2 kilometres from the first. Path and shore reconvene below tall pines at Calfclose Bay. This is the best picnic spot on the walk and, as a result, very popular.

Keep along the shore to the next point, which has fine yew trees. An obvious made path now leads towards the long white houses of Stable Hills, then skirts them to the right and joins their drive. Where this swings right, a gate on the left leads to a path through swampy woodland (The Ings). In 300m this does a ninety-degree left turn and heads for the open again at Strandshag Bay. Don't count on having this to yourself. It's a handsome spot, though the view of Friars Crag and the north-western fells may well seem familiar even if it's your first visit. It must be one of the Top Five Lakeland views. (I'm as guilty as the next photographer).

The minuscule detour to Friars Crag, after the next gate, is hardly to be missed. Now simply join the crowds of strollers along the track back to the landing stages. This may be the shortest walk in the book, but you'll still have walked a lot further than most of them.

A good way back to the town centre from the landing stages is via Crow Park. Go through a gate in the railings opposite the new theatre. The obvious path ahead leads back to the shore, but half-right a fainter line goes over the crest of a rise. Follow this and keep straight on to the far corner of the field. Enter the lane and go right; follow it round past the caravan site and then the Rugby Club and straight ahead to the bus station.

*The shores of Derwent Water near Barrow Bay*

# Walk 7: Beautiful Borrowdale to Derwentwater

Seatoller to Keswick

| | |
|---|---|
| Introduction | Borrowdale is a perennial favourite among Lakeland dales, but poses certain problems for car-borne visitors. Even supposing they can find a parking space, satisfactory circular routes can be hard to find. As Borrowdale also has the best bus service of any of the valleys, the solution is obvious. A linear route makes it easy to traverse the full length of the valley, guaranteeing an outing of rare diversity: fellside, woodland, riverside, pasture and lakeside all figure. As a bonus, the route finds the easiest of all approaches to the superb viewpoint of Castle Crag. This is the most exciting part of the day, but there is pleasure, albeit less dramatic, from start to finish. |
| Character | The walk is on clear paths and tracks throughout, with one very short stretch of road. The ascent and descent of Castle Crag are steep but elsewhere the gradients are mild, with much level ground. |
| Distance and Time | 9 km/ 6 miles, 250 metres/ 800 feet of ascent. Allow 3 hours, or a lot longer if you intend to fully appreciate the views. |
| Refreshments, etc | Cafe in Seatoller. The Borrowdale Gates Hotel is the only source actually on the route but there are several cafes in Grange, reached by a short detour. And then there's Keswick... |
| Local Base | Keswick, Seatoller, or anywhere in between. |
| Local Transport: | Bus 79 Borrowdale Rambler from Keswick to Seatoller. The service is virtually hourly until early evening, year-round, half-hourly in high summer. There is also one later bus, except on Sundays. |

**The Walk:** The sharp constriction of the valley between Grange and Rosthwaite is still occasionally referred to as the 'Jaws of Borrowdale'. Sensitive 18th-century travellers drew the blinds on their carriages

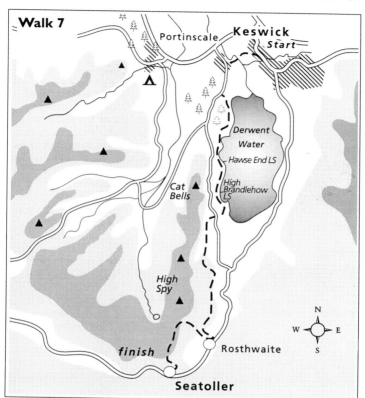

**Walk 7**

Portinscale — Keswick — Start

Derwent Water

Hawse End LS

High Brandlehow LS

Cat Bells

High Spy

finish — Rosthwaite

Seatoller

N / W / E / S

when they passed through here, such was the awe engendered by the steep slopes, or perhaps by overblown descriptions in some of the guidebooks of the time. Blinds are not an option on today's bus, but the modern traveller appears to be made of sterner stuff. Seatoller is the end of the line, so there's a dedicated space for the bus by the entrance to the car park. Cross the car park to a track rising from its far end. After a gate fork left on a gently rising green track. Pass through a second gate then keep bearing left to swing round under a magnificent yew tree with a ruin just below. Continue on a narrow sheep-track, rising slightly through bracken, then almost level to meet

*Seatoller village, start of the walk*

an obvious stony track coming up from the left. There are fine views of the valley head and the hanging valley of Comb Gill as well as glimpses of the rooftops of Seatoller.

Continue through another gate. The track seems to be aiming straight for Honister Pass but then there's a junction with a large cairn and yellow arrow: go right on a green path, up to a gate, through it, and and then alongside the wall. The path soon levels out: Kings How appears, then Castle Crag. Descend slightly to a footbridge over Scaleclose Gill and continue, with minor undulations, over another footbridge (Tongue Gill). Now the path rises gently to a broad col with some wire sheeppens. Ahead, crags frame a view of Derwent-water and Skiddaw. Bear right immediately on a narrow little path which wriggles round below a small crag. Ignore the first stile and keep the wire fence on your right until it ends. Now go over it by a small stile then over the wall by a big one and up to the right.

A huge heap of quarry spoil rises ahead, with a well engineered but steep path up its left side. The gradient eases at a terrace with old workings to the left: these are interesting to explore if you have the time. The main path to the summit continues to their right through larches.

The summit has a platform above a war memorial plaque, but encroaching trees mean this isn't the best viewpoint in either direction. The classic view to the north is from a spot about 50 m to the east, where the ground drops off steeply to the treetops below. Probably the best view over Rosthwaite and Stonethwaite is obtained lower down, from the terrace above the heap of spoil.

Reverse the ascent route to the base of the spoil, then find a ladder stile behind some pine trees - this is not the same one crossed on the ascent, being about 50 m further east.

Go down to the left, getting quite steep and somewhat eroded, through a gate then zig zag down through woods. You'll need to put the brakes on to avoid crashing into a stile as you reach the level valley floor. Go left on a broad stony track, which soon dives into dense woods.

The main track doesn't follow the river, but there are several obvious opportunities to wander across to it. It may seem tempting to follow the river-bank throughout, but this involves a couple of passages of awkward scrambling. One highlight of the main track is a small quarry working on the left: a five-second detour reveals an arch and some amazingly multicoloured rock.

Just beyond this go up over bare rock to a huge cairn. A more open area gives a view back up to Castle Crag. 50 m further on, the track bears left and then forks. Take the right fork, up to a signpost then back right ('Grange'). Descend gradually and finally come along-

*Castle Crag*

side the river. Unfortunately the road is close on the other side. The track runs level then over a slight rise to a gate and down to a foot-bridge, which seems quite unnecessary except in the very wettest weather. Just before the bridge another track joins in from the left, which is where you would have come down if you'd carried straight on from the col before Castle Crag.

The river makes a sweeping bend, past some alder trees with their feet in the water, then the track diverges, past a vehicle barrier. There's a campsite on the left, then another camping field on the right. At a track junction bear left, up to Hollows Farm and through the yard (or stop for Bed and Breakfast). Continue on an obvious track through an area strewn with agricultural implements.

Follow the track through fields until it swings left. At this point go right to a gate - not the smart one marked 'private no path', but the field gate just right again. A narrow thread of path curls past a holly-tree and boulder in intimate embrace. The prominent crag across the valley, beyond the rooftops of Grange, is Black Crag.

The path slips down to the road near the Borrowdale Gates Hotel. Go left along the road for about 600 m. Just after crossing over Ellers Beck there's a gate on the right with an old green sign: 'Public footpath to Lodore'. The path crosses a field with many rushes. After the second kissing gate the path forks. Take the left one (the right fork leads to Lodore) then at another fork keep right, across a mix of bog and brack-en, to join a clear path with a long run of duckboards. Go left. The head of the lake is just to the right. The duckboards may be an intrusion, but without them this stretch would be a lot more 'interesting'.

After a few hundred metres it's back into woodland, where the ground becomes a lot firmer underfoot. The main path is clear, though there are innumerable variations on the lake side. Joining a tarmac drive by a cottage (The Warren), go right for 100 metres or so then leave it where it swings into the private grounds of Abbot's Bay. Follow a path close to the shore, past Brandelhow. The main path goes over the next little peninsula, while a variant goes round the shoreline.The two variants rejoin just before a landing stage (High Brandelhow). You can, of course, catch a launch back from here, but the walking is so easy and so delightful you'll surely want to continue.

Stroll on through the trees, or along the shore, to a second stage (Low Brandelhow). Just past this the track forks. The right fork seems the obvious way but only leads onto the promontory enclosing Otterbield Bay. Left is the shorter way. After 500 metres there's a sign informing us that the main track leads to Lingholm and Keswick.

However, it's easier to slant right to a gate, beyond which the last bit of shoreline can be followed to Hawse End landing stage.

This is the end of the lake-shore walking, which makes it a good place to catch a boat back to Keswick, but if you do want to keep hoofing it, refer to Walk 5. Or you can catch one of the anti-clockwise launches as far as Lodore and finish by Walk 6, or catch another bus there and do the whole thing all over again.

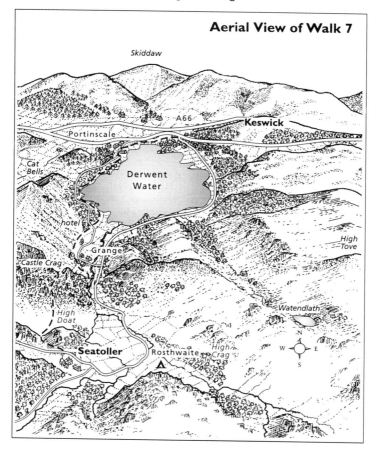

**Aerial View of Walk 7**

# Walk 8: Beyond the Chocolate Box

*Keswick to Watendlath and Rosthwaite*

| | |
|---|---|
| *Character:* | Moorland paths on the promenade above Walla and Falcon Crags, valley tracks to Watendlath, and a stony final descent to Rosthwaite. This, and the crest of Walla Crag, are exposed to bad weather. Navigation should be child's play, except on the way off Walla Crag, which could be tricky in mist. |
| *Distance and Time:* | 13 km/ 8 miles, 500m/ 1700 feet of ascent: allow 5½ hrs. Use of the free bus from Watendlath (summer Sundays) saves 2½ km/ 1½ miles, 60m/200 feet of ascent, or about an hour |
| *Refreshment:* | Apart from the start and finish, there is a seasonal cafe in Watendlath. |
| *Local Base:* | Keswick or Borrowdale. |
| *Local transport:* | Bus 79 Borrowdale Rambler from Rosthwaite to Keswick; the service is virtually hourly until about 6 pm, with one later bus, and runs year-round. On summer Sundays there is a free National Trust bus from Watendlath to Keswick. |

A succession of set-piece views is the main theme of this route. Some of them already adorn a thousand chocolate boxes and mint-cake wrappers, but the others are just as good. You'll enjoy them all the more as they are less hackneyed, not to mention less crowded.

**THE WALK:** From **Keswick Market Place** go to the right of the Moot Hall and at Fishers large outdoor shop turn right, down Lake Road. Go through the subway and continue down past Crow Park to the landing stages.

Just past a small toilet block on the left a public footpath leads through **Cockshot Wood** and continues as a fenced-in path across fields. Cross the road and go up the steep slopes of Castle Head, slanting to the left. A direct course is uncomfortably steep and will only disturb the squirrels. As the main track eases, paths on the right lead up to the rocky summit, with views well worth the five-minute detour.

Rejoin the main track and take another confined path across a field to Springs Road. Turn right and follow it past suburban villas to Springs Farm. A track rises to the right of a beck. At a junction, take the right branch, signposted 'Rakefoot Farm, Walla Crag, Castlerigg Stone Circle'. Reaching the edge of the wood you can see Walla Crag ahead and the steep edge of Falcon Crag beyond. Go up past a communications mast and keep straight on. Cross the stream, join a narrow lane, and go to the right, past **Rakefoot Farm**.

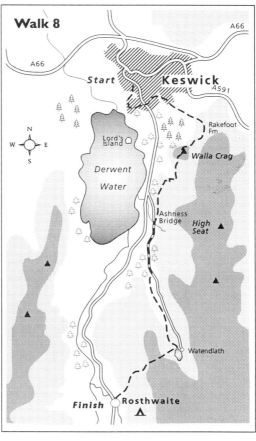

Cross a footbridge, near three fine pollarded ash-trees. Go on up rough tracks and climb up to the right when open fell is reached. Where the way levels out, crossing a small beck, take the narrower right branch through a gate near a bend in a wall and then follow a path close to the steep edge of the crags. On a fine day with a westerly breeze, this is a popular area for launching paragliders. I have counted eight in the air at once. The best views of Derwentwater, Bassenthwaite and Skiddaw come before the summit of Walla Crag, while the summit itself introduces Borrowdale and the high central fells.

Recross the wall and go down beside it until a clear track forks left. It soon forks again, and this time take the right one, which curves away on a roughly level course, around the head of Cat Gill and then just above the summit of **Falcon Crag**. It's well worth a brief detour to this summit. With its steep rock face out of sight but certainly not out of mind below, it's an airy perch, with unobstructed views north and south.

The path then crosses a rocky slope below broken crags, descending gently and then more steeply. Ashness Bridge soon comes into view; descend alongside Ashness Gill to reach it.

**Ashness Bridge** is a notorious 'honey-pot', but why? We have already seen better views, with more to come, and there are prettier bridges. The main answer is historical. In the early days of tourism there were clear rules as to what was 'picturesque'. Ashness Bridge clearly has all the desired elements. It just needs a few jovial peasants driving shaggy cows across the bridge. In those days true devotees looked at the landscape in a mirror or 'Claude Glass' to ensure that it was correctly framed. The modern equivalent is probably the screen of a Viewcam. Another factor, today, is that while there are finer views and more attractive bridges, you can't drive right up to them.

Continue, either on the road or through the

*Ashness Bridge*

woods to its left. At Ashness Cottage it becomes necessary to follow the road for a short way. Re-entering woods look for paths on the right and go up towards Surprise View. This is almost as well-known and frequently snapped as Ashness Bridge, so it's not much of a surprise to most people. However the crag edge is unfenced and the well-worn rocks can be slippery, so the wrong kind of surprise is always possible.

There is no need to walk on the road, but keep fairly close to it for about 350m until you reach an obvious track on the right, opposite a passing place. Follow this through the woods to meet Watendlath Beck. Go through a gate in the wall ahead then right to cross a footbridge. There is an unusual direction sign set in the ground; take the path on the left. A steep craggy hillside across the valley has a long central wall of clean rock: this is Reecastle Crag, which has some short hard rock-climbs.

The path continues alongside Watendlath Beck, across the base of Caffell Side, all screes and tumbled boulders. One yew tree by the path has found a cunning way to prop itself up. The path crosses some bare rock slabs which - especially when wet - show up some fine fragmented inclusions. The way is obvious until the very end, where keeping close to the beck is best. This brings you to **Watendlath Bridge**, arguably a better example of the genre than Ashness Bridge, if only because it doesn't have tarmac across it. Cross the bridge to enter the hamlet.

In summer Watendlath is usually boiling with people, many with a faintly puzzled expression as if not quite sure what they are doing there. Despite Watendlath's high reputation, there really isn't much to see, though you can ponder on how a real house can be the home of a fictional character.

A bigger puzzle is why so many people flock here when so few have read the books - Hugh Walpole's 'Herries Chronicles'. Have you? More puzzling still is why anyone would want to drive here, especially when there's a free bus: the narrow dead-end road is absurdly congested. Watendlath is already a prime case for Park and Ride; Heaven help it if they ever make a TV version of the books, though they'll probably film it in Yorkshire. T'North's all t'same to some people. For us the main attraction may be the availability of refreshments (watch out for the chaffinches).

To continue to Rosthwaite, recross the bridge and go along the shores of the tarn; where the track forks take the right one, which rises steeply ('Bridleway to Rosthwaite'). A short ascent leads to an open, hummocky ridge: on your right is the charmingly-named Puddingstone Bank, and ahead is a fine view, improving as the descent steepens to reveal the level green fields of upper Borrowdale. At the head of the valley is Sty Head Pass, with craggy Lingmell behind, Great Gable to its right and Scafell Pike further back on the left. Closer is the rough mass of Glaramara, with the deep glacial hollow of Combe Gill scooped out of it.

Descend quite steeply towards a dark spruce plantation then swing left on an eroded path. Keep on past a gate in the wall on the right., with a slate slab declaring that it leads to 'Keswick and Bowderstone'. At a second gate, the corresponding slab is currently broken but enough remains to deduce that Stonethwaite is ahead, while we go right to descend to **Rosthwaite**. A clear track descends to join a pretty walled lane and comes down to the river (Stonethwaite Beck); cross the bridge and reach the road exactly at the bus stop.

With perfect timing, you've just missed one bus and it's almost an hour till the next one. Rosthwaite is a few metres up the road, the village shop being met first. There is a tea-room off to the right, while a few metres up the main road are two hotels. The Royal Oak is not licensed for non-residents but has tea and scones in the afternoons, while a very few metres further on is the Scafell Hotel's Riverside Bar. Muddy boots are not so much tolerated here as almost de rigeur.

*Above the final descent to Rosthwaite, looking to Borrowdale and Great Gable*

# Walk 9: The Not-so-ugly Sister: A Traverse of Skiddaw

*Bassenthwaite to Keswick*

| | |
|---|---|
| *Character:* | A high-level fell-walk, but mostly straightforward. The Ullock Pike ridge is generally easy, the steepest section being the final rise of the Pike. There is an awkward section on steep loose ground on the final approach to Skiddaw. The descent is uncomplicated. The upper reaches are extremely open and exposed to bad weather. There are well-marked paths throughout. |
| *Distance and Time:* | 14¹/2km/ 9 miles, 900m/ 3000 feet of ascent. Allow 7 hrs |
| *Refreshments:* | Nothing en route |
| *Local Base:* | Keswick. |
| *Local Transport:* | Various buses pass Bassenthwaite, including 555 Lancaster - Carlisle, 73 Caldbeck Rambler (73A goes the long way round), and X4 Keswick - Workington. The X5 Keswick - Workington service goes the wrong side of Bassenthwaite Lake. |

Skiddaw may be the least glamorous of the Lakeland 3000-footers (914m just doesn't have the same ring) but glamour is superficial. From some angles it is the most beautiful of the 'Threes', and it stands alone in a way that none of the others can match. Its long level summit ridge gives me a greater feeling of altitude than any peak in England. The Victorians - or their beasts of burden - used to carry hampers of quail and crates of champagne up here, but on any half-decent day the air and the sense of vast space are better than the finest Bollinger.

As to the specific route, a short bus-ride from Keswick opens up a splendid traverse. The Ullock Pike ridge is widely considered the best route onto Skiddaw, while the Tourist track, tedious in ascent, provides an easy descent allowing full enjoyment of the panorama. The final stretch, round Latrigg and into Keswick, will surprise many and delight most, not least because it avoids traffic all the way into the town centre.

**THE WALK**: Just to be confusing, the walk doesn't actually start

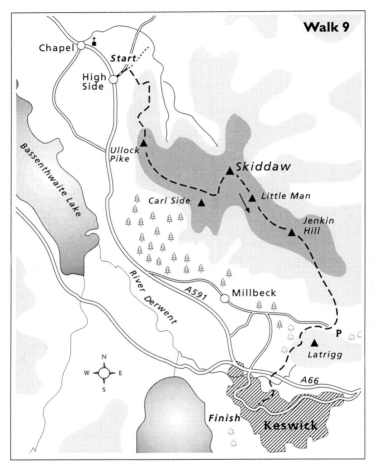

from Bassenthwaite at all (lake or village) but from the bus stop at High Side. And just to be even more confusing, this is not the same stop as used in the Bassenthwaite to Keswick low-level walk (that being Chapel Crossroads). High Side is a small cluster of houses just over the crest of a long drag which starts soon after the previous stop

*Derwent Water from Skiddaw Little Man*

at Ravenstone.

Walk up the branch lane ('Orthwaite 3') for about 500m. Just past a small parking area is a gate on the right with a bridleway sign. Go straight up the track for about 200m then sharp right alongside a line of gnarly old hawthorns. About 100m past these turn left to a ladder stile and keep straight ahead to a second stile; 50m past this swing right on a green furrowed track.

The first stile has good views back over Bassenthwaite, both lake and village, while by the second Skiddaw is beginning to loom as a great lumpen mass, in contrast to the elegant ridge of Ullock Pike.

The next gate leads onto open fell. The track continues, without loss of height, parallel to Southerndale Beck. As the main track swings left to cross the beck a less distinct branch bears right and climbs to a heathery col below Ullock Pike. From the col simply follow a clear path up the ridge, rising in waves with a final steeper haul to **Ullock Pike**.

The ridge to Ullock Pike is known as The Edge, which prompts comparison with other edges, like Striding, Swirral and Sharp. Terms like 'knife-edge ridge' are bandied about in print, often giving the reader no clear idea what is meant - one sometimes wonders if the writers are any the wiser. Perhaps it's time we had a clear grading system: something like this: knife-edge - possible to fall down either side: airy -

feels possible to fall down either side: narrow - possible to see into the valley on both sides. And so forth. Under this classification Sharp Edge might just count as a knife-edge, Striding Edge is merely airy, while - despite the definitive ring of its name - The Edge is never better than narrow. Still, there is a fine sense of elevation, especially looking north over the lowlands.

Ullock Pike completes the major climb of the day, but don't open the champagne just yet; Skiddaw still has something up its sleeve. Try not to let it prey on your mind. The next descent is trivial and the succeeding climb onto Long Side is gentle. This section has a fine aerial view of Lakeland's bayou country, the swamps around the Derwent delta at the head of Bassenthwaite Lake.

The path spurns the summit of Carl Side and heads directly for the main event. Skiddaw's appearance from here may well have you wishing to put off the evil moment. For the dedicated collector of 'Wainwrights', too, Carl Side is easily snapped up in a ten-minute detour. However, **Skiddaw** is neither as big nor as steep as it looks. It's a 200-metre ascent from a muddy puddle glorying in the name of Carlside Tarn. The path swings left onto bare slopes of slate fragments. Mostly a simple, soulless trudge, it steepens toward the end and crosses over into the realm of definite grovel. A patch of bare rock relieves the monotony and gives better traction. The labour is almost but not quite over at this point. The slope above is convex, gradient easing with every stride.

The ridge is gained near a large shelter but the summit itself lies 300m further north. This may seem inconsiderate but the view is worth it. It's even better if you venture another 150m, to the very end of the ridge. There is an unobstructed prospect northward, over fertile lowlands to the Solway Firth and, if it's clear enough, far into Scotland. To the east are Skiddaw Forest and the northern Fells, sweeping round to the unfamiliar back of Blencathra, but for the most part this is not really a Lakeland view. For that - well, wait and see.

Return southward along the full length of the summit ridge, a good 500m from the trig point. Ample supplies of stone have been turned into shelters, which are marginally more useful than the usual rash of cairns. At the south end of the ridge bear left, just as Derwentwater comes into view, to begin a steady descent on a broad stony track. Below the steepest part the main track goes ahead through a gate but unless the weather has done the dirty it is far better to veer right, following the fence, and head on up to **Skiddaw Little Man**. This is a Lakeland view, and one of the best. It feels as if the whole of Lakeland is laid out below, though this is obviously not true. In fact Derwentwater is the only lake on show.

The view is just as good, if not better, from the cairn on Lesser Man, which is hardly more than a pause in the descent. From here slant left, on a fairly steep path, to rejoin the tourist track. This rolls on down over the broad slopes of **Jenkin Hill** and through a gate where the scenery starts to change. Derwentwater drops out of sight behind Latrigg while on the left the little glen of Whit Beck, decorated with larch trees, draws attention to Helvellyn.

The descent is steeper hereabouts and the track is a broad untidy scar, but then this has been a popular route for well over a century. Imagine large parties of respectably-clad Victorians or Edwardians, usually accompanied by guides and often with ponies carrying picnic hampers and probably some of the travellers too. Perhaps it's a good thing ponies have gone out of favour, or Skiddaw might now be the highest peak in the Lakes. For many years there was a refreshment hut near the gate, but even its remains are now hard to find.

A level stretch follows, with grass underfoot: a welcome relief. Near its end is a beautifully carved stone cross commemorating the 19th-century Skiddaw shepherds Edward and Joseph Hawell. We should resist the tendency to scatter memorials all over the hills, but if anyone deserves to be remembered like this it must be those who lived and worked on the fells. From here it's an easy five minutes down to the car park at the road-end below Latrigg.

The car-park is often full, except when it's overflowing. Don't be too inclined to envy those whose walk will end here; most of them will have slogged up the same route you have just descended. And they will miss the discreet charms of the final descent into Keswick. Go through the car-park to a gate on the left ('Bridleway Keswick').

The path descends at a lovely steady gradient but is initially hemmed in between the steep side of Latrigg on the left and a plantation on the right, limiting views to sporadic narrow glimpses of distant fells. Causey Pike is the most recognisable. The plantation ends at **Round How** with a sudden view over Derwentwater and the north-western fells. I almost didn't mention this. If you like surprises, don't read the previous sentence. The descent continues at the same relaxing gradient through taller trees, getting a little steeper as Keswick comes into view - and the A66 into earshot.

Keep right on, but don't miss the hippos, just before the bridge over the A66. The pleasingly-named Spoony Green Lane lands you in suburbia at Briar Riggs. Go left, and where the road narrows look for a footpath on the left behind a hedge. This continues, crossing a side lane, still parallel to the road, to a gap on the right above a mini-roundabout. Cross here and aim towards the pyramidal glass roof of **Keswick's** Leisure Pool. Go round the left side of the pool building and down to the road. Go right at once, through a gate in iron railings and down the steps into Fitz Park, then diagonally across grass, avoiding the cricket square, to an iron footbridge. (If there is cricket in progress go round!) Cross the bridge and follow the lane until faced with a one-way sign. Go the 'wrong' way, always a pleasure, then cross the main road and the large car park, beyond which various ginnels lead through to the market place.

## Walk 10: Lakeland's Only Lake:

*Bassenthwaite to Keswick*

| | |
|---|---|
| *Character:* | Generally level walking by field paths and quiet lanes, with one steep climb and gentler descent on forest tracks. The lake-shore section may be impassable when the water is very high: this can easily be avoided but the walk is better if it can be included. |
| *Distance and Time:* | 12 miles/19 km; 1000 feet/300m of ascent. Allow 6 hours |
| *Refreshments:* | Pub in Bassenthwaite, near the start: a surfeit in Keswick. En route only the tearooms near Mirehouse and these are seasonal. |
| *Local Base:* | Keswick. |
| *Local Transport:* | Various buses pass Bassenthwaite, including 73 Caldbeck Rambler (73A goes the long way round), 555 Lancaster - Carlisle, X4 Keswick - Workington (the X5 Keswick - Workington service goes the wrong side of Bassenthwaite Lake). |

More than most, an explorer's walk. Despite its generally low altitude and proximity to villages and roads, it is full of the unexpected. There is further proof of the principle that it isn't a tourist attraction if you can't drive to it. St Bega's church is one of the most charming and historic in the District, but usually quiet and serene. Other highlights are a close look at the District's only lake and a grand view from the slopes of Dodd.

**THE WALK:** The bus stop is at Chapel Bridge crossroads; **Bassenthwaite village** is 500m up the lane to the north, but the walk heads down the lane opposite, signposted to Scarness. Turn off right through a gate with a white fence, follow a track and keep straight on through a gate with a yellow arrow, to the left of a house. Cross the garden and turn left down the drive, which leads out into a lane. Immediately past the entrance to Bassenthwaite Lakeside Lodges turn down a track to the shores of **Scarness Bay**.

The next section may be impassable when the lake is very high: you'll find out soon enough. (If so, it is necessary to return to the lane and follow it for about a kilometre until the other route rejoins).

From Scarness Bay the path follows stiles and waymarks across fields then tracks the lake-shore around the blunt promontory for about a kilometre until it reaches the swampy corner of Bowness Bay, which is far quieter than its namesake on Windermere.

While we're mentioning Windermere, why is Bassenthwaite the only Lake in the Lake District? Because it is. All the others are meres or waters. 'Lake Windermere' is a tautology, though possibly not quite as offensive as Lake Ullswater or Lake Coniston. What next? Mount Scafell Pike? Borrowdale Valley? Three Shires Inn Pub?

Let's return to the walk before I lose the plot entirely. Keep straight on where the Broadness Farm track angles left. Cross marshy fields via duckboards and a footbridge to rejoin the lane. Leave it again, after little more than 100m, by the next footpath on the right. Go straight across three fields, through a small mixed wood (Woodland Trust) and then through a second wood mostly of larch. On leaving this, **St Bega's church** comes into sight.

The isolated position of the church raises an obvious question, to which no definite answer is available. St Bega herself came from Ireland in the seventh century, landing at St Bees, which also preserves her name in a corrupted form. Parts of the building may predate her, and chunks of it are definitely Norse in style. A leaflet is available in the church for more information, and donations to its upkeep can be made.

Leaving the Church, go up to the edge of a wood and follow it along to the right; continue along the track to an iron gate leading into

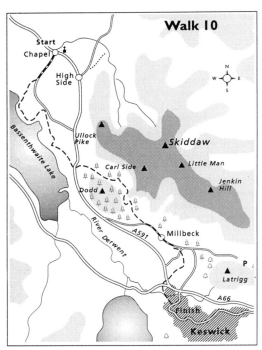

**Walk 10**

Start
Chapel

High
Side

Bassenthwaite Lake

Ullock
Pike

Skiddaw

Carl Side

Little Man

Dodd

Jenkin
Hill

River Derwent

A591

Millbeck

Latrigg

A66

Fitush

Keswick

the grounds of Mirehouse. There are plenty of signs here to indicate which ways are private, which for paying guests and which for mere walkers.  Even without payment you get a fair view of the house - which looks vaguely Scottish - and a good impression of its grounds. The route leads out to the road and straight across to a car park, where the **Old Sawmill Tearooms** also serve Mirehouse - buy tickets here if you want to see the house and grounds properly.

The one and only climb of the route now lies ahead, but if visibility is even half decent it will be  worth it. Follow red and green markers across Skill Beck and up a steep forest road overlooking it. Intermittent views of Dodd summit through the trees give a measure of progress, which may be either encouraging or depressing. Half-way up a path breaks away left - watch for the red and green markers. This route is less direct - and therefore less steep - and a bit more varied, but if you've got the bit between your teeth you might prefer to steam straight on up the road. The two routes rejoin just below the sharp col of Long Doors (Door, with variations in spelling, is a frequent Lakeland term for a col or pass).

Just before the top the track forks, the right branch being signposted to Dodd summit. A steep  muddy path climbs to this summit. The views are restricted by trees, but there is a good overview of

Bassenthwaite Lake. Return the same way - which, by simple deduction, will tell you that this bit is optional.

The left branch of the path goes over the top to reveal a fine view of Keswick, Derwentwater and Borrowdale. As it swings away to the right Helvellyn is added to the prospect. Pass one track branching left then, at a four-way junction overlooking Bassenthwaite Lake, take the track sharply back left. This rises slightly before resuming the business of descent. After crossing **Scalebeck Gill** it becomes narrower and descends more steeply.

After a few minutes the path forks: take the narrower path on the left across a beck and up a few metres to a gap in a wall. It descends on the far side, first beside the wall, then slanting left across the slope to run just above a plantation. A stile and footbridge then lead to a lane which is followed into the village of **Millbeck.** The lane ahead is just as entertaining as the footpath which runs parallel (reached down a lane on the right). The architecture of Millbeck is quite diverse and the fronts of the houses probably more interesting than the backs.

Just before Applethwaite is a poignant war memorial. Take a narrow road down to the right and along to a T-junction. Almost opposite is a track, to the right of a house called, with exceptional accuracy, Field View. Cross the beck by ford or slate bridge and take the path on the right. This runs alongside the stream at first then bears away left.

Cross a smaller beck by a footbridge and stile then follow the wire fence on the right, round a corner and down towards an iron-clad barn. Angle slightly left to the opposite corner of the next field then resume the previous heading. The path is on stilts across a wet patch. Go up to cross the A591 and straight on between the houses: the hedge on the right may bark loudly at you. Go diagonally left across a field to where a stile and footbridge lead to the crossing of the A66.

Go under the old railway line at a narrow arch and left across a field, aiming towards the left end of the white buildings of Keswick School. A narrow hedged path leads into the school drive and this in turn opens into a suburban road. Go down a short way then first left into Glebe Close. An iron gate on the right gives access to a path linking to another street. Go down to a junction of major roads near a modern slate church. Cross the first road and then bear left, alongside the River Greta, towards the town centre. At the first mini-roundabout, the bus station is two minutes walk away to the right while most of **Keswick's** cafes, pubs and gear shops lie straight ahead.

# Walk 11: The Best of Blencathra

*Mungrisedale to Keswick*

| | |
|---|---|
| *Character:* | A steep climb on the east ridge of Bannerdale Crags is the most strenuous part of the day, albeit easier than it looks. Most of the walking is easy, with grass underfoot, though parts of the descent off Blencathra are steep and eroded. The final stage into Keswick is on easy paths and tracks. Navigation is easy, though the talented could probably manage to get lost coming off Bannerdale Crags in cloud. |
| *Distance and Time:* | 15 km/9$^{1}$/2miles, 770m/2500 feet of ascent. Allow 6$^{1}$/2 hrs |
| *Refreshments:* | Pub at Mungrisedale (don't get excited about Birds' Bistro: it's strictly for the birds), nothing else till Keswick. |
| *Local Base:* | Keswick. Also Penrith (see Local Transport notes) |
| *Local Transport:* | Bus 73A Caldbeck Rambler, twice daily from Keswick, every day from late July to the end of August, and on Sundays to the beginning of October. Otherwise Saturdays only. The clockwise service 73 takes over an hour to reach Mungrisedale. X4/X5 buses between Workington, Keswick and Penrith pass the end of the Mungrisedale road, adding about 3 km/ 2miles of easy walking. This is a half-hourly service throughout the year (less frequent on Sundays), which makes Penrith a viable base. |

Blencathra is a big complex hill and the popular circuit via Hall's Fell and Sharp Edge only samples one quarter of it. The swooping summit ridge - possibly the best in the Lakes - really cries out for a traverse, but the walker tied to a car faces a long and tedious plod to complete the circuit. As a liberated linear walker, for the same effort, you get the fine eastern approach to Bannerdale Crags as a starter and the unexpected delights of Brundholme Woods for afters. And  you still have the option to include Sharp Edge in the itinerary.

**THE WALK:** From the acute bend in the road in **Mungrisedale**, walk down a track past a red phone box. There is a footpath sign to Mungrisedale Common. After 200m a gate leads onto open common. A landrover track runs up the valley, parallel to the **River Glenderamackin**. Bowscale Fell rises on the right, the Tongue directly ahead and Souter Fell on the left. Bannerdale Crags soon appear between Souter Fell and the Tongue, but Blencathra itself is hidden, and will remain so for some time.

The track crosses Bullfell Beck by a small footbridge; 50m past this, take the path on the left, still following the River Glenderamackin. The path gains height painlessly on bracken-clad slopes just above the stream. The river's course is incised, a valley within a valley. Ahead Bannerdale Crags become increasingly dominant with the east ridge facing us, throwing down the gauntlet.

Use stepping stones to cross a wet patch then splash across Bannerdale Beck by the ruins of a weir. Immediately take a smaller path up the knoll on the right, the base of the east ridge. After a brief respite there is another steep grassy climb, the path an obvious parting in the bracken. A scattering of rocks signals the end of the steep bit and you emerge onto an almost level green spine.

The upper ridge puffs its chest out trying to look really steep, but it's all bluster and it soon lies back. The climb is enlivened by the colourful surroundings, with two-tone slate spoil and plenty of heather and bilberry. The remains of some old workings are obvious around the half-way mark. Scramblers may find patchy enjoyment on the crest but all difficulties can be avoided on the left, though never too far left. There is no need to go anywhere near the nasty scree gully. With a little guile you can complete the ascent without using your hands.

At the top of the ridge there are good views (any excuse for a breather) back over the Glenderamackin, Mungrisedale and the Eden valley to the distant Pennines. Swing rightwards, skirting the edge of the crags. The first cairn, with its upright slate slabs, isn't the summit, which is 100m further west. Blencathra makes a grand entrance like some Wagnerian diva.

From the stacked slates of the summit cairn steer for Skiddaw (a little north of west) until a narrow path materialises. Lope down this to the broad grassy saddle at the head of the Glenderamackin. Let your momentum carry you straight on up the other side, swinging left along a well-defined edge.

As the slope eases slightly, **Sharp Edge** is seen in profile. Should you suddenly feel the urge, a small cairn here marks the start of a

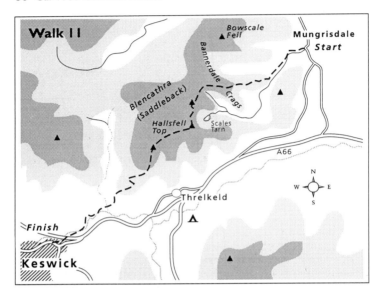

contour path which runs below Brunt Knott to join the usual path up to the Edge.

Otherwise, continue steadily upward. There is a brief levelling before the final pull. This brings ten minutes of toil with a very abrupt ending. Now keep right to the cairn on **Atkinson Pike**, then make a beeline, past two crosses of white quartz (one very much older and better made than the other) and a pool in the dip, to Hallsfell Top, the summit of Blencathra. The final approach is over deceptively mild grassy slopes, making arrival at the summit a dramatic moment.

The top is perfectly poised at the head of **Hall's Fell** ridge, with an aerial view of Threlkeld. Thirlmere and Helvellyn lie to the south and the view sweeps round to Derwentwater and the north-western fells. Best of all, a wonderful scarped ridge swirls away to the west, a boundary line hung in the sky: to the left is Lakeland, all rocks and trees and water; to the right is 'Back o' Skidda', all smooth and gold and brown.

Exhilaration makes this ridge seemingly effortless, the rise to the sharp pike of Gategill Fell Top barely noticed. Keswick comes partly into view. Then there's a swoop down to Blease Fell and a last slight

*Blencathra in winter*

rise. The path gets momentarily lost in grass but reasserts itself, with cairns, as the slope ahead steepens towards Keswick.

The descent gets steadily steeper: the worst section is crying out for some engineering, or just common sense. At the bottom of this, the main path veers left but a cairn marks the start of a fainter path breaking away to the right. This connoisseur's alternative weaves away across the moor until, above a steep drop into the Glenderaterra valley, it swings sharply left in a distinct groove. Carry on down along the edge of the bracken until above a car-park. A grass path through the bracken now offers a direct descent but those who value their knees will take the longer route, rejoining the other path near the bottom.

By the cattle grid at the lower end of the car-park is a kissing-gate. A path descends into the grounds of the Blencathra Centre (a former Sanatorium). It heads to the right, joining the main track, with helpful yellow arrows, then continues as a narrow path again. Follow this through more kissing-gates into a larch plantation, then cross the next field diagonally, to a stile into a lane. Go right along this to Derwentfolds and a footpath sign on the left just before the house. Go down the track under the oaks and into a dell (no other word for it) with a footbridge over the Glenderaterra.

The path slants up a steep bank to join a semi-tarmac lane. Follow this up right, then left where it forks, to a gate. From this go straight ahead on a descending tarmac lane for 500m to a permitted path dropping sharp left into the woods. Double back right almost at once,

*Blencathra traverse: walkers on Gategill Fell Top*

then run a fairly straight course down to the **River Greta**. Although the A66 is nearby, the river muffles the noise beautifully. All too soon, steep slopes force a climb back up again, followed by a generally level section high above the water. As the path loses contact with the river, continue for about 300m to a small signpost. Caravans in view beyond the river also identify this spot. Drop back left towards the river and go upstream 100m then up to join the old railway line and follow it over a bridge.

All that remains is to follow the course of the railway, now a foot- and cycle-path, for nearly two kilometres to **Keswick's** old railway station, now substantially transformed and far too posh for the likes of us. There is a campaign to re-open the railway line, which would be a wonderful thing, even if it meant re-routing the finish of this walk, but it won't happen before this book comes out.

A pyramidal glass roof identifies Keswick's Leisure Pool. Go round the left side of the pool building and down to the road. Go right at once, through a gate in iron railings and down the steps into Fitz Park, then diagonally across grass, avoiding the cricket square, to an iron foot- bridge. Cross the bridge and follow the lane until faced with a one-way sign. Go the 'wrong' way up the street, cross the main road and the car park, beyond which various ginnels lead through to the market place.

# Walk 12: The Noble Art of Bog-trotting

*Keswick to Ambleside*

| | |
|---|---|
| *Character:* | This is a long and surprisingly arduous walk, but there are plenty of escape routes. Parts of the route, notably around High Seat and High Tove, are always wet. In hot weather, those with a sense of fun may be happy to accept wet feet, but there's a long way to go afterwards and a spare pair of socks might be a good idea. Waterproof boots and gaiters are an obvious alternative. Gradients are easy but the bog-trotting sections are strenuous in their own way. The ground is mostly grassy, getting stonier towards the end. Navigation is easy as far as High Raise, but from here to Sergeant Man and Blea Rigg there could be uncertainty in mist. |
| *Distance and Time:* | 32 km/20 miles, 1200m/ 4000 feet of ascent. Allow 12hrs. Descending via Easedale to Grasmere saves 6 km and about 700m. |
| *Refreshments:* | Nothing en route, except bilberries and muddy water. |
| *Local Base:* | Ambleside, Grasmere, or Keswick. |
| *Local Transport:* | 555 LakesLink buses run regularly between Windermere and Keswick, seven days, year-round. |

Wainwright's 'Central Fells' is full of phrases like 'extreme dreariness' and 'shockingly wet'. Obviously Wainwright was not in touch with his inner child. Bogs can be fun, both physically and mentally. Real enthusiasts will be disappointed; there's far less proper bog on this route than Wainwright suggests. By Dark Peak standards this isn't a bog-trot at all, barely even a bog-sprint. The only decent bit is a short section after High Seat and all the soggy fun is over before Ullscarf.

The rest of the route involves nothing more exciting than ordinary walking, but with great views, as you'd expect from its position at the very heart of Lakeland.

**THE WALK**: From Keswick Market Place go to the right of the Moot Hall. After 200m turn down Lake Road, through the subway and past Crow Park to the landing stages. Just past a small toilet block on the left take a footpath through **Cockshot Wood** then a fenced path across fields. Cross the road and climb steeply, slanting left, onto Castle Head. As the main track eases, paths on the right lead to the rocky summit, if you can spare five minutes.

The main track leads to another confined path across a field to Springs Road; turn right to **Springs Farm**, then up a track to the right of the beck. At a junction, take the right branch, signposted Rakefoot Farm, Walla Crag, Castlerigg Stone Circle, up past a communications mast and straight on. Cross the stream, join a narrow lane, and go right, towards Rakefoot Farm.

Cross a footbridge and follow rough tracks through a gate onto open fell. Keep left, parallel to the beck but well above it, on a good grassy track. This swings right as the slopes open out, but a green path keeps straight on and nearly level, still roughly parallel to the beck, to a ruin.

Bear left and follow the beck along the left side of heathery Low Moss. The path crosses the beck several times to maintain a firm footing, reaching a sheepfold before the ground steepens. Maintain direction along a narrow path, then bear left on a faint path through shorter heather to avoid steeper ground ahead. The path becomes clearer, with stony patches, as it steepens, then eases onto firm grass again.

Swing round right and up a broad sloping shelf, keeping to grass. Climb to the right of a rash of rocks, then up on a clearer path to a large cairn with a good view of Derwentwater and Bassenthwaite. Now go left on a broader but slutchier path to the top of **Bleaberry Fell**, with a shelter and several cairns.

A clear path winds across a moor with several pools, crossing the first minor bogs. A wire fence and rudimentary stile lie athwart the path before a wetter section. Climb through a band of rocks then up again to a trig point on the rocky turret of High Seat. If getting here has whetted (wetted?) your appetite, the next kilometre will be pure joy.

Bear left to another wire fence, crossing it at a stile. Hasten down firm ground towards beckoning mosses and peat hags. There is enough of a path to prove that we aren't the only mad buggers around, but it dissipates at the finest section of bog. There are two main approaches, devious or kamikaze. For the latter, old clothes (or none) are advised. Some people pay good money for a mudbath, others get it free with exercise and fresh air thrown in.

The devious may try crossing the fence again but further convolutions are required. At the next angle of the fence, cross back to the

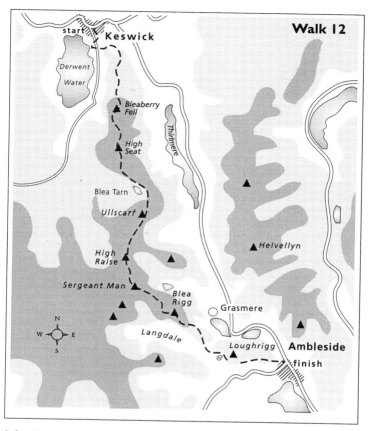

**Walk 12**

*start* — **Keswick**

*Derwent Water*

*Bleaberry Fell*

*High Seat*

*Thirlmere*

Blea Tarn

*Ullscarf*

*High Raise*

*Helvellyn*

*Sergeant Man*

*Blea Rigg*

○ Grasmere

N
W E
S

*Langdale*

*Loughrigg*

**Ambleside**

*finish*

left side - avoiding a lethal stile - then leave the fence to cut off the corner. The path rises fractionally to **High Tove**. A sizable cairn with a protruding pole, not at the exact highest point, overlooks the path to Thirlmere. Slant back towards the fence and plough on.

Though pleasantly splashy, the next descent lacks thrills and spills. Rocks are encountered around Middle Crag. Old iron posts lead over Shivery Knott before rejoining the newer fence. The next, nameless, rise is marked by a trident of inverted fence posts. The fence bears left as Blea Tarn appears below and right. Crossing a level area, swing left to avoid some pools and drift back to the fence as the ground rises and rocks reappear. Cross the fence to an outcrop with an iron post then make a roughly level traverse to meet the fence again just before a gate (left to Thirlmere, right to Watendlath).

Follow the left side of the fence towards Standing Crag. Climb left of the main crag then right above the rocks to meet the fence again near the crest of the crag, a fine retrospective viewpoint. The slopes of **Ullscarf** are broad and almost arid, their few pathetic excuses for bogs not worth trifling with. The fence is followed till it turns sharply right on rocks. Bear left here, following iron posts, to the small summit cairn.

Windermere comes into view for the first time and Grasmere appears as you start the descent, still following iron posts. These become more scattered but the path becomes clearer. A level area has some decent bogs but curiously the path avoids the best ones. Descend rockier ground to **Greenup Hause**. The way down left is to Thirlmere via Wythburn, or Grasmere via Far Easedale. Descending to the right leads via Greenup Gill to Rosthwaite in Borrowdale.

Go straight on up an obvious path, alternately peaty and stony, to a big cairn on Low White Stones. Level ground and easier climbing lead to another cairn before the final slopes of **High Raise**. The trig point and shelter are on the western edge of the plateau, above steeper ground, with a fine view of Bowfell, Esk Pike and Great End beyond the deep trough of Langstrath. Southward, Harrison Stickle and Pike o' Stickle look odd from here, as if undergoing a trial separation.

Wander southeast across the plateau, passing a small tarn and the remains of a fence. **Sergeant Man** soon appears, the most prominent of several rocky excrescences. It's another of Wainwright's inconsistencies to count this a separate fell, yet ignore worthier peaks like Ladyside Pike and Little Stand. Still, its rocky top is a fine viewpoint.

Descend left, briefly steep and eroded, then follow a stony track across a small beck and on down a broad knobbly ridge. Near a flat rock slab we get our first view of Easedale Tarn and the most obvious path drops down and left towards it, with Grasmere beyond. (This option is worth considering if energy or daylight are ebbing: it's still a bumpy twelve kilometres to Ambleside.)

Keep straight on across a vague saddle (good view of Stickle Tarn and Pavey Ark from its far side) to a path running level onto the hummocky top of **Blea Rigg**. A prominent cairn on the left after 300m is not the official summit, which is lower. When Easedale Tarn reappears, Wainwright's summit is just ahead on the right, but if you're not bothered and want an easier passage, bear right through a broad notch then round left on a green path, faint but with cairns, overlooking Langdale. This soon rejoins the stonier main path.

Dip and rise to **Great Castle How**. Rydal Water appears ahead. You may reflect that Ambleside is beyond it. After Little Castle How comes a more definite, right-slanting descent. The path levels and swings back left but there's a great view of Langdale from just to the right. Cross Swinescar Pike on gentler slopes, passing a prominent cairn. Dropping down again, bear right and pass to the right of a bog with central pool, below Lang How.

Climb again slightly, with more views of Langdale. Descend once more, level out, then look for branch paths left to cross a small beck in a V-shaped valley, which gets much steeper just below. Traverse left on a steep slope, overlooking Elterwater quarries, to a green saddle with a large cairn. Follow the crest of the ridge ahead or the easier path alongside, converging as the ridge narrows. From the peak of

*Sergeant Man, seen from Blea Rigg*

Dow Bank, directly above Elterwater village, descend steeply right at first then back left to a saddle and over more slight rises. The dips have stepping stones, if your standards are really slipping! Go down again steeply and then bear right, meeting the road as high as possible.

Go left past **High Close Youth Hostel.** In another 50m there's a wooden gate in the wall on the right. Go down left on the gravel path, then right and left at successive junctions and out to the road. Those desperate to go over Loughrigg need to go left 30m, then refer to Walk 12 (Volume 2), reading backwards.

Otherwise follow me down to the right for 400m to a track on the left at a right hand bend; follow this easily round above **Loughrigg Tarn**, a beauty spot all the more beautiful for its lack of car-parks. On a good day the view to the Langdale Pikes should amply compensate for the absence of bogs.

Go over a stile on the left by a hollow ash. The path runs across fields to join a stony track. A short steep climb precedes a level traverse below **Ivy Crag**. Where the track splits take the left branch up to a shoulder with a bench, looking back to the Langdales, Wetherlam and Great Carrs.

Swing left up a shallow valley. Keep to the main path, trending right, levelling out then dipping to a ford before a slight final (and I do mean final) rise to a col. The rooftops of **Ambleside** can be seen at last. Simply follow the track ahead and down for about a kilometre, finishing with a steep twisting descent, to meet the Under Loughrigg road.

Go right for a few metres and over the bridge across the Rothay. Fork right to cross Stock Beck, then take the middle of three paths across Rothay Park, below the church, and into a street leading to Compston Road at the heart of Ambleside.


# Walk 13: The Great Ridge

*Bridgend to Grasmere over The Dodds and Helvellyn*


From Great Dodd to Dollywaggon Pike, over 10 km, the Helvellyn ridge never drops below 750m except, just barely, at Sticks Pass. The traverse gives the most sustained high-level walking in the Lakes. Getting up naturally takes a little effort, but the route used is as easy as any and has an interesting start, making use of the climbers approach to Castle Rock. Once up, the walking is easy and the views are great.

| Character: | A lot of high-level walking, potentially exposed to bad weather, but in general the going is easy. The initial climb is steady and after this gradients are mostly gentle. There is grass underfoot most of the way, the stoniest section being the beginning of the final descent. The first climb is pathless but it's hard to get lost, and on the ridge there should be no problems in navigation. |
|---|---|
| Distance and Time: | 20 km/ 12½ miles, 1250m/ 4100 feet of ascent, from Bridgend to the Travellers Rest. Allow 9 hours, though hardened fell-walkers should be well inside this time. Continuing on foot into Grasmere village adds 1½ km/1 mile to the distance and nothing to the ascent - in fact it's downhill. |
| Refreshments: | Nothing at the start or en route, but there is a spring (Brownrigg Well) about 300m just south of west from Helvellyn summit. |
| Local Base: | Grasmere (Windermere, Ambleside and Keswick are also convenient) |
| Local Transport: | Regular bus service 555 links Ambleside, Grasmere and Keswick, almost hourly throughout the year. |

**THE WALK:** Get off the bus at **Bridgend**, just south of the dual-carriageway. Walk down a traffic-free lane opposite the Thirlmere road, and into a car-park. Opposite the toilet block a path leads to the road: cross, climb wooden steps, then follow a rising track round and up to the top left corner of the field. There is a basic footbridge over the leat, which diverts the waters of several gills to Thirlmere, which supplies Manchester.

**Castle Rock's** North Crag towers overhead as you climb up alongside the wall. It's only 60m high and only just overhanging, but on both counts first impressions may be different. Surprisingly, the climbing is mostly middle-grade stuff, nothing really hard by modern standards: the holds are just too good.

At the base of the crag cross the fence on the left. Go up the climbers' descent route until it scrabbles up into a steep gully. Go left again, below a holly, then up easy rocks avoiding a patch of scree, to a

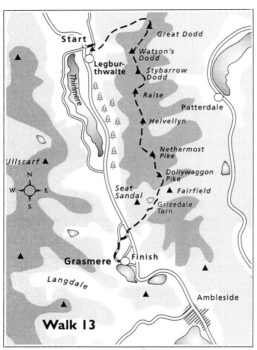

Walk 13

sheep-track under steeper crags. Where these fall back rightwards, bear left to a grass-and-bracken shoulder overlooking the first ravine of Mill Gill. A path traverses to the base of the upper ravine. Cross the Gill - stepping stones may be slippery - and escape up the opposite side.

The Gill itself is a recognised scramble but graded 3(S), for experienced scramblers and dry conditions only. There is a fairly clear path alongside at first, presumably the scramblers' descent. Eventually the ravine broadens into what Wainwright calls an amphitheatre. You may even see Christians being thrown to the lions.

There is no further excitement, just a broad grassy slope. Navigation is elementary: up. Resist the temptation to go too fast; fresher legs will enjoy the rolling miles ahead. For variety, try going up backwards, which varies the muscle action and allows you to enjoy the expanding views. In spring and summer skylarks, often several together, provide mood music. Try to disentangle the melody lines. Eventually there's a cairn in the middle of nowhere. This puzzled Wainwright, but is obviously there to mark a patch of rocks, though they mark themselves perfectly well.

Another cairn on the skyline is not the summit, just Little Dodd. Sorry. The true summit is ten minutes further. Once this is reached, even with sixteen kilometres still to do, you begin to feel that the fat lady is loosening her vocal chords. It's certainly a good place to rest and rehydrate. A massage with scented oils would be nice, too.

The next stretch, to **Watson's Dodd**, is ridiculously easy, if you can remember how to walk downhill. 'Depression imperceptible' says Wainwright. Miserable bugger. 'Exhilaration perceptible', surely: just look at that ridge unfurling ahead.

The main path avoids Watson's Dodd, then spurns the exact summit of Stybarrow Dodd, but now you're up here it seems silly not to tick them off. If you're going to tell folks that you did the Dodds and Helvellyn, you ought to do the Dodds. Otherwise, why not miss out the summit of Helvellyn too? Why not miss them all out? Why get off the bus at all?

A level track rejoins the main path, and climbs gently to **Stybarrow Dodd**. As the climb steepens, the path trends right, but keep straight on. The actual highest point is debatable, but a scrappy cairn with large upright stone will do as well as anywhere, and from here it's an easy stroll to a larger cairn to the west. Go a few metres further for a better view over Thirlmere.

The descent is, briefly, unexpectedly steep: not precipitous, just a hint of ruggedness ahead. Two huts and a ski-tow - little used in recent mild winters - are prominent on the north-east slope of Raise. **Sticks Pass** is the lowest point before the descent to Grisedale Tarn. There is some soft ground as you start to climb again, best avoided well to the right or by waiting for a drought. As the ground rises, rejoin the main path, which becomes a stony scar, winding through bands of pumice-like rocks. The path, for once, heads directly for the summit of **Raise**, the rockiest top on the ridge.

The path onward to White Side is obvious and the innumerable cairns utterly superfluous. The average spacing is about 15m, but visibility would need to be less than 2m before the path became hard to follow. Who builds these cairns? It's a complete waste of energy, though some people say that about walking in general.

If it's even vaguely clear, keep to the left, above the slopes falling into Keppel Cove. In fact, 'keep to the left' could become a litany from now on. The western slopes are relatively smooth, while the eastern flanks are carved into crags, gullies and ridges. During the Ice Ages, winds tended to accumulate snow on the more sheltered north and east facing slopes, which thus became more heavily glaciated.

**White Side** is a very easy ascent. Dropping down again to the next col, Helvellyn Lower Man looks formidable ahead. To the left,

Catstycam can look almost vertical (it isn't): to the right, Brown Cove Crags are the only major crags west of the main ridge. They have good scrambles and winter routes but aren't steep or smooth enough for rock-climbing.

The ridge of Lower Man proves less steep than it looked: hands are not needed. Still, it's the steepest climbing since the start of the day and as close as we'll get to real mountaineering. The summit has little identity on three sides but does give a grand view back to the north. An easy

*Striding Edge in wintry conditions with the Helvellyn summit ahead*

stroll leads on to the plateau of **Helvellyn** itself.

The first landmark is the large cairn above Swirral Edge. Then comes the trig point. The actual highest point is marked only by a cairn, no bigger than many that litter the paths. Just south is a cross-wall shelter. The best seats are always taken: is there a booking system I don't know about? 200m beyond this, what looks like a stumpy cairn carries a memorial plaque. Eroded paths drop towards Striding Edge, but we contour round, past the heads of two gullies, to a rocky promontory. This is a quieter lunch spot than the summit area, and a good place to observe antics on the Edge.

Stroll on to the next col, one of the few places where the ridge is narrow enough to look down both sides simultaneously. Beyond, the path trifurcates; keep left then wander across a level plateau strewn with spiky rocks, one of which is the summit of **Nethermost Pike**.

Carry on over the negligible rise of High Crag then down along the edge, looking down to **Hard Tarn** on its ice-scoured shelf.

From the next col there is a steeper rise on the edge of crags. From the cairn above it's a five-minute amble to the summit of Dollywaggon Pike, though the largest cairn is once again not on the highest point. The view tilts southward now, with Windermere, Esthwaite and Coniston Water all in evidence.

Starting the descent, the very steep edge of Falcon Crag defines a shoulder ahead. Aim for this: the main path joins briefly but slopes off right again, determined to avoid all excitement. If - and only if - it's misty, it might be prudent to follow its stony zig-zags down to Grisedale Tarn. Otherwise descend by easy stages to an obvious perch thrust out to the east overlooking Grisedale. Venture a few metres down from the highest point for impressive views down the gullies.

Swing back right towards the tarn, crossing a patch of scree, then left again when grass is reached. Just down to the left, below some small outcrops, is the head of another imposing gully. A mostly grassy promontory, above Tarn Crag, separates this from a final deep gully. Go down from its head - away from the gully! - on a ribbon of grass between screes. Swing back left when the screes run out. With a few more artful swings you can stay on grass all the way down to the crossing path just above **Grisedale Tarn**.

Pass just below the outlet of the tarn, on very soft ground with stepping-stones. The path runs close to the eastern shore then gradually rises away from the water across a steep slope. It's mildly annoying to arrive at Grisedale Hause slightly above its lowest point, but a major consolation that this is the last climb of the day (unless you count the stairs on the bus). Look at the path on the left, grinding up to Fairfield, and spare a thought for Skyline Walkers.

The descent is initially fairly steep, on a restored path, then levels out alongside Hause Moss. The Vale of Grasmere comes into view, still some way below but in sight at last. Another steeper descent follows, with more restored pitches. Cross the gill below some pretty cascades and rattle down a final repaired section before the gradient eases right off.

Beyond an isolated enclosure, drop down to a small waterworks intake and cross the gill by a footbridge. A broader track now provides a foolproof finish. **Grasmere** (lake) appears and, much nearer and of more immediate interest, the Traveller's Rest. On reaching the main road, if you fancy walking all the way back to Grasmere, go straight across. A quiet lane under Helm Crag leads to Easedale Road on the village outskirts. Otherwise, turn left alongside the road. The pub appears at once, about 200m away, and the bus stop is another 100m further on.

## Walk 14: Above Ullswater  Fry THIS

*Pooley Bridge to Glenridding*

| | |
|---|---|
| *Character:* | Generally easy walking, with hardly any steep gradients, over a mixture of fields, woodland tracks and clear hill paths, plus a few short stretches of road-walking towards the end. Navigation is straightforward. Several stretches can be soggy in wet weather, so decent boots are recommended. |
| *Distance and Time:* | 15 km/ 9 miles, 290m/ 950 feet of ascent. Allow 5$^1$/2 hours |
| *Refreshments:* | Both Pooley Bridge and Glenridding have pubs and cafes. Refreshments are also available on the lake steamers. There is a basic cafe below Aira Force, just off the route. |
| *Local Base:* | Pooley Bridge or Penrith |
| *Local Transport:* | Bus Service 108 (Patterdale to Penrith) runs 8-9 times daily from mid-April to end-October, 3 times on Sundays and Bank Holidays. Winter services are less frequent, with none on Sundays. The bus stops at Pooley Bridge steamer pier, where the walk starts.<br>An obvious alternative is the Ullswater Steamer from Glenridding to Pooley Bridge. The full summer service (roughly hourly) runs from April to the start of October, with a more limited but still useful service for about a month either side. |

This walk is bound to be compared with No. 15 (Howtown to Glenridding) and probably wins on points. Longer, but with a fraction less ascent, it is easier underfoot. It is also guaranteed to be less busy. The walk runs the full length of Ullswater, giving greater variety of surroundings and views. Much of its course is nearly level, 300m above the lake, and the extra altitude adds distance, depth and drama. Aira Force and Wordsworth's daffodils should tip the balance. But you can't make up your mind till you've done both.

**THE WALK:** From **Pooley Bridge** pier walk left - no footpath - for 100m. Watch for an inconspicuous sign on the right ('Path Waterfoot'). A small permissive path rises above the road. Follow this to the junction with the A592 and cross to a gate by a large beech tree then go left along the edge of the fields. Just above a bend in the road go right on a rising track, with a green waymark and an Environmentally Sensitive Area sign. 300m up, by a gnarled ash, join the dots left across the field, into a wood with many young ash trees.

The path ascends painlessly through the woods, with frequent glimpses of the lake. Double back over a stile and after 200m double back again near the crest of the ridge. Traverse open brackeny slopes with a view across to Howtown and a first glimpse of Helvellyn. These are occluded by a plantation as the way levels and starts to descend, but Blencathra and Carrock Fell compensate.

After another stile the ground ahead drops more steeply, revealing a fine pastoral foreground: bear right, avoiding the drastic descent. Keep to the right edge of the next field then turn left on a tractor track near a barn. Follow this down to cross Ramps Beck. 'Ramps' is an old name for wild garlic, which still blooms here in May, as your nose will confirm. Just below the crossing is a wooden sluice, running down to an old mill.

Just before Wreay farm go right through a gate and up to the top left corner of the field. Go left down a lane to **Bennethead** and keep straight on, following signs for Matterdale. 250m past Bennethead, just after a right hand bend, keep a sharp lookout for a footpath sign and kissing-gate on the left, partly masked by the hedge. The sign, embedded in a tree-stump, points to another kissing-gate. Keep straight on to a third then bear right across a low-lying field, skirting wet patches, to a gate and stile (yellow arrow) at the far end under oak trees. 100m further on, the right of way has been diverted. Keep left of a small barn to a stile, then on to a footbridge 50m right of a nearly-dead tree and ahead to a wooden gate.

Cross the lane to a kissing-gate ('Footpath Aira Force'). A stony track runs down below a mass of gorse, levels off amid bracken then rises, narrower now, to the right. The short climb brings the first real outcrops of rock and some prickly moments in gorse before the way levels off at a broad saddle. From the far end of the saddle the path swings right and clings to a contour around the head of the valley and into the plantations of Swinburn's Park.

Spruce and larch interrupt the views for the next kilometre, though claustrophobia is unlikely. As the path emerges into the open it rises ahead, narrow and precise, past cascades and an unexpected footbridge. After this excitement it settles down to a roughly level course around the slopes of Gowbarrow Fell for another kilometre. There is only one fork, where the lower, clearer left path is taken. This swings back right to reveal a perfectly-composed view towards the head of the lake, backed by the Helvellyn range. The best vantage point of all is a large cairn on a rocky rise above **Yew Crag** (known to climbers as Gowbarrow Crag).

The way now slides gently downhill across a steep slope then descends more steeply above a curious castellated house called Lyulph's Tower. Although a lot of height has been lost, we are still a useful 50m above the lake.

At a path junction go right and slightly up to a gate, through this and right on a manicured path, arriving in a few minutes at **Aira Force**. The most direct line leads to the footbridge above the main fall, but it's equally easy to drop down to another bridge below it.

Cross the lower bridge and climb the steps, then go through a gate into a field and up the path rising to the right into a plantation. Go through this to a small car park and the A5091. Go down the road, enjoying another fine view of Ullswater. Helvellyn is hidden now, so St Sunday Crag takes pride of place. At a bend, after 400m, take a footpath to the right, through a clearer area between trees and past a power-line pole to cross a beck in the corner of the field. Go through the left of two gateways, currently gateless. Follow the fence on the right through the next gate and on to a stile under a magnificent oak tree. Take a green track through the rushes then slant a little left at a marker post. Pass another post, cross a stony track and go over a stile into an alder wood. The beck is usually just a splash. Keep fairly straight past more posts and another beck to the road. Go along this for 150m to the end of the wooden fence then 50m further to a thin path which follows the lake shore into woods.

For most of the year these are fairly ordinary but for a few weeks in March/April they are a major attraction, for this is where those daffodils were, and still are, located The delicate wild daffodils are vulnerable to the 'it can't hurt to take just a few' mentality. You will be lucky to be 'lonely as a cloud' here today. How closely you follow the shore for the next few 500m depends on several factors: aversion to road walking, persistence, and, most significantly, the level of the lake and/or enjoyment of paddling. Crossing the beck where the road bends is more of a wade than a paddle, while Glencoyne Beck 200m on could be more of a swim than a wade. All but the pathologically stubborn will resort to the road for the next 250m, after which there's a good path on the left.

The main path keeps close to the road but after passing a boathouse the shore can be followed in preference. Unless you're Ranulph Thingy Whatsit Fiennes it's back to the road for 150m where the steep Stybarrow Crag almost shoulders it into the lake. Then escape left again by an engineered path. Steps rise to a small bluff with pines and a view, then the way is level again, through conker woods, to another set of steps, another bench and another view. Finally join the road just by the **Glenridding** sign. Count your blessings (verges and a 30 mph limit) for the last 300m into the village.

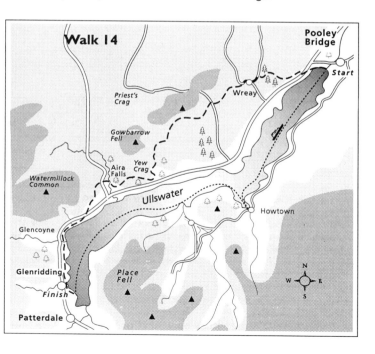

# Walk 15: Top of the Pops

*Howtown to Glenridding*

| | |
|---|---|
| *Character:* | Belying its reputation, this is more a woodland than a waterside walk. A glance at the map might suggest that it's flat, too. In fact the cumulative effect of its repeated undulations could be a shock to the unprepared, and stony paths are no fun in pumps or slingbacks. |
| *Distance and Time:* | 11 km/ 7 miles, 300m/ 1000 feet of ascent. Allow 4 hours Deduct 1¹/₂ km/1mile (but no ascent) if you get a bus back from Patterdale instead of returning on foot to Glenridding. |
| *Refreshments:* | In Glenridding, on the boat, at Side Farm towards the end of the walk and in Patterdale just before the finish. |
| *Local Base:* | Glenridding or Patterdale. Both are easily accessible from Penrith. Basing yourself in Pooley Bridge means making two cruises on the lake. Is this a bonus? |
| *Local Transport:* | Ullswater Steamer from Glenridding (or Pooley Bridge) to Howtown. The full summer service (roughly hourly) runs from April to the start of October, with a more limited but still useful service for a month or so either side of this. There is a summer-only bus service from Bowness. |

This is the best-known linear walk in the Lakes, included in several books of otherwise circular walks. Being best-known does not make it the best - it has many rivals in these pages - but it is a grand outing.

Ullswater is many people's favourite lake. Its windings produce several dramatic changes of perspective, from gentle rolling country around Pooley Bridge to the lake-head overlooked by St Sunday Crag and Helvellyn.

**THE WALK:** From the bus stop in Glenridding walk over the bridge and then under the arch of the Glenridding Hotel. The hotel allows us to cross its territory out of pure altruism completely unconnected with the fact that we pass between its bar and coffee shop. Stride on through the hotel car park to join the spur road leading to the pier with its large car-park.

The Ullswater Steamers 'Raven' and 'Lady of the Lake' are long and low in the water, giving quite a feeling of speed, especially on the fore-deck. The actual speed is about 10 knots, to which all powered craft on the lake are restricted. The occasional bionic canoeist may go faster. In the absence of jet-skis and similar abominations, the lake is popular with kayakers, sailors and rowers. There is always action and the half-hour journey to Howtown passes quickly.

From the jetty go right, over a footbridge. The sign says Public Footpath Sandwick - no mention of Glenridding. Follow the shore to a kissing-gate, where queues are likely unless you were first off the boat. Continue between shore and flower-meadows (both out of bounds) to another kissing-gate then along the lane for 80m. A gate on the left has a slate sign for Patterdale and Sandwick. Climb steeply, with some wooden steps, then through yet another kissing-gate (osculatory fatigue is a hazard on lowland walks). Turn right on a level but narrow path - overtaking can be tricky here - which emerges into an open brackeny area with a good view back towards Pooley Bridge.

This elevated position is savoured briefly before descending again towards shore level. Meander along through woods mostly of oak. The path reaches open fields overlooking the lake at Sandwick Bay but veers away almost at once.

Cross a bridge into the quiet hamlet of Sandwick, bear left past

*Hallin Fell and Ullswater*

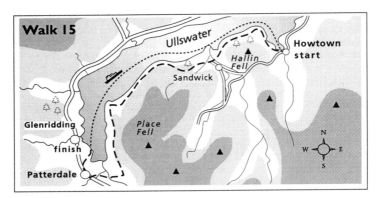

pretty Townhead Cottage and then right on a bridleway. After a short climb, dip to a wooden footbridge below Scalehow Force. (To see the falls properly requires a ten-minute detour). From the bridge there is another short steep climb but the way drops down again almost immediately. The path can't settle to one level but undulates continually through woods now dominated by birch. Clearings allow intermittent views, different each time.

A more level stretch across a steep slope arrives at **Silver Crag** and a definitive view of the lake head, backed by St Sunday Crag and the long line of the Helvellyn ridge. This is a tempting spot for picnics, paddling and general loitering, but take note that the best path to continue on is at the same level as before.

There is a final irritating haul up to a shoulder with pine trees then the path descends gradually. A splendidly mossy-roofed barn is directly opposite Glenridding pier, but the walk still has legs. Keep straight on, past a campsite to enter the yard of Side Farm under a magnificent sycamore. Turn right (sign for Glenridding). It would take considerable willpower to go past the tea rooms across the yard. In summer you can sit outside and watch swallows darting in and out of the barn.

Continue down the farm track to the road. Patterdale village is only about 200m to the left, but for **Glenridding** turn right. There is no pavement this side at first. Pass the Mountain Rescue HQ, an impressive building, especially considering that Mountain Rescue services are dependent on voluntary contributions. Beyond this a permitted path gives a little shelter from the traffic, passing a giant redwood. When it comes back to the road near the head of the lake, cross over to another permitted path above the road. This returns to the road just outside Glenridding village. An obvious path opposite leads past the boat hire/ tea shop and then pleasantly along the shore back to the pier.

# Walk 16: Not the Fairfield Horseshoe

*Patterdale to Ambleside*

| | |
|---|---|
| Introduction: | The Fairfield Horseshoe is an obvious and immensely popular circular walk. The symmetry of the two ridges makes a pleasing picture on the map and a commanding one in reality (the best place from which to see them is a boat on Windermere). But, at the risk of being heretical, doesn't that symmetry make those ridges, and especially the out look therefrom, just a little too much alike? For the same effort the liberated walker can enjoy the best of the Horseshoe - the long, loping descent with its vast prospects over Windermere to Morecambe Bay - and take in another grand fell, St Sunday Crag. Already it feels like two walks for the price of one. An unfamiliar start from Patterdale and the exciting approach to Fairfield by Cofa Pike are icing on the cake. |
| Character: | A good honest fell-walk. The ground is mostly grassy with a few rockier sections. Navigation is simple in good visibility, but in mist the section between Arnison Crag and St Sunday Crag requires care. In very bad visibility some care may also be required between Fairfield and Hart Crag. Cofa Pike is steep and rocky but demands no real scrambling. There are some soft patches on the descent which can be very muddy at times. |
| Distance and Time: | 16 km/ 10 miles, 1100 metres/ 3600 feet of ascent. Allow 7 hrs |
| Refreshments, etc.: | Nothing en route; shop and pubs at start, choice at the finish. |
| Local Base: | Patterdale or Ambleside |
| Local Transport: | Bus service 108A Kirkstone Rambler from Bowness to Glenridding: get off at the Patterdale Hotel. This service runs three times daily in high summer only, plus Saturdays, Sundays and Bank Holidays from early April to the start of the high season. Patterdale does have a year-round bus ser vice, but only from Penrith, which is two bus rides from Ambleside. |

**The Walk:** Walk a short way south down the road, through the 'narrows' by the **White Lion**, then take the track on the right, past the public toilets. This curls round to the right and then a footpath, with a low sign, cuts off to the left across a marshy area with young birch trees. Follow the path to a gate in a wall but don't go through; instead climb up to the left, alongside the wall. This is fairly steep, but rests can always be taken on the pretext of admiring the view back over Patterdale village and the head of Ullswater.

Not very far up there is a small crag. Well-worn rock and trampled ground show that it is frequently used by some of the many outdoor centres in the area. Above this, the path becomes less distinct but the wall is a handy guide. Where this breaks off to the right on a more level course, continue in the same line on a narrow sheep-track. Just above and left is a rocky knobble. This is **Arnison Crag**. As far as Wainwright is concerned this is the top, and no connection to other fells is offered either. In fact it clearly isn't even the highest point on this ridge, though it is the best viewpoint.

Scramble up, then return to the sheep track. This angles across a shallow col, an oasis of grass amid acres of bracken. The next little lump can be avoided on the left, which is where the track takes you anyway. The rise beyond that is the summit of the fell; the best way to tackle this is straight up the front, zig-zagging on grass to avoid patches of rock. Bracken still reigns to either side.

Drop down slightly to the right and pick up another faint sheep-track which slides back leftward. This track, faint though it is, gives the best way along the remaining hummocky ridge to Trough Head. This is a crossroads of indistinct tracks; keep straight on, past a long boulder lying low in the grass. The path gradually becomes more distinct, often running in a distinct groove which suggests it may be of some antiquity. It rises gradually across the broad southern slope of Birks.

Where it crosses a small stream, a cairn may prove a bit of a red herring. Don't go straight across: the dim track on the other side soon peters out. Instead go up the stream a short way until the clear grooved path resumes its leftward progress.

As the slope ahead eases, just below Gavel Moss, the path starts trying to lead you across, level now, to cross Coldcove Gill. It's certainly possible to do this, reaching St Sunday Crag via Lord's Seat and Gavel Pike, but it is easier to break off right at this point. Skirt north of Gavel Moss, keeping to slightly higher, rockier ground, and keep straight on until you reach a broad clear path - the 'trade route' from

Birks to **St Sunday Crag**.

Almost at once this starts climbing steeply, over rocky but easy ground, in two great steps. The slope drops off steeply to the right into Grisedale, but there's no real view of the craggy north-west aspect of St Sunday Crag. This is the home of some classic easy climbs and scrambles, especially Pinnacle Ridge, widely regarded as one of the best scrambles in the Lakes.

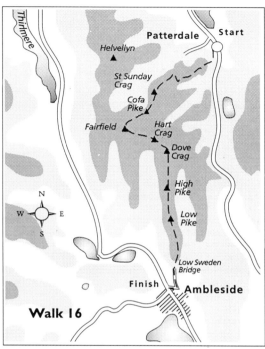

The gradient eases, leaving a ten-minute plod over stony ground to the summit. As summits go there's nothing wrong with it but it's perhaps a little disappointing for such a fine-looking fell. The ridge runs on south-westward and the views gain in depth as it narrows. The slopes dropping into Deepdale are especially steep. Beyond the bowl of the valley head rises the tangled north face of Hart Crag and Fairfield. There are some classic rock-climbs on Hutaple Crag, and the whole area gives some fine winter routes. In the other direction, this ridge gives probably the finest view of the east side of the Helvellyn range. Apart from Eagle Crag, low down in Grisedale, this has little to tempt the summer rock-climber, but it's the most reliable and popular area for winter climbing in the whole of the district.

After a few minor ups and downs, the ridge drops to Deepdale Hause. A cairn and clear path descending to the right offers an escape

*Hart Crag and Fairfield seen from St Sunday Crag*

route, well worth considering if the weather should deteriorate seriously. From Grisedale Tarn the shortest descent is to Dunmail Raise (bus service but no shelter) and it's also possible to descend via Tongue Gill to Grasmere - see Walk 13 for more details.

If soft options are spurned, continue straight ahead to the sharp rise of **Cofa Pike**. This can look quite formidable; scramblers will call it a walk, but some walkers may call it a scramble. Confident walkers can play the Cofa Pike Game. Here's how it goes; everyone starts with 100 points. Deduct one point each time you take your hands out of

*Cofa Pike*

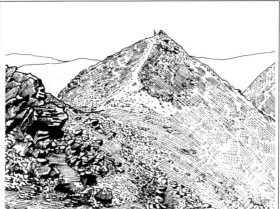

your pockets, 5 points each time you actually touch rock. Using one trekking pole forfeits 50 points, using two forfeits 100 - though you can still win as the rules allow for negative scores. And if you're tempted to take risks, bear in mind that if you fall and hurt yourself you'll be disqualified. 99 points is a fair score as far as the summit of Cofa Pike. The game is a bit more challenging on the short

*Looking north from Fairfield's summit towards Helvellyn*

continuation ridge, and in wet conditions most players will sacrifice points liberally here.

While we're in the mood, we may as well make a direct run at the short rocky step onto **Fairfield** proper. Beyond this there's just a clear stony track leading directly to the summit, with its scatter of cairns and rough shelters, none of which are very effective when the wind is really blasting across the plateau.

From the summit, head south-east at first, keeping the steep drops close on the left, to the head of a steep gully with the alarming name of Flinty Grave. The track then runs almost due east before swinging south-east again and dropping more steeply to the slight col of Link Hause. From here there's a short but steep climb onto Hart Crag.

A little care is needed in mist on the rocky descent that follows: the branching path to Hartsop above How can appear more obvious than the main route. Watch for cairns, and if still in doubt steer south-south-east. After the first descent, a ruined wall appears on the right, marking the end of all navigational problems.

Follow the wall, which becomes more impressive, first down, then up the gentle climb to **Dove Crag** and on down very easily to High Pike. A few peaty patches and pools lurk to catch those who wander along with eyes only for the distant views.

The rise to **High Pike** is negligible, the drop on the other side isn't. Gaps in the wall may tempt you to cross to the right (west) side, but there's no real advantage in doing so. The track on the right is peaty and soft: you wonder how ground so steep can hold so much moisture. It's as if gravity were some newfangled idea that hasn't really caught on.

There are more boggy patches on the way to Low Pike, and on the descent beyond. Keep an eye out for a path which swings sharply left about 100 metres below the Pike. This soon curls back right to run below and parallel to the ridge and wall, thereby avoiding the awkward rock-step at **Sweden Crag**. You can always return to the ridge, in pursuit of stereo views, but soon the two paths reunite anyway.

There are scattered trees around now. The path, always clear, keeps steadily on down, with Ambleside and Windermere ahead, then makes a couple of zigs and zags down the steeper drop to **Low Sweden Bridge**. Just beyond this is the farmyard of Nook End, beyond which a surfaced lane runs all the way down into Ambleside, past the campus of Charlotte Mason College. At the 'T' junction onto Smithy Brow, the main road is just below to the right. Much more attractive, the Golden Rule pub is a few metres up to the left.

# Sources of Information

## In Print

All the bus, train and ferry operators produce printed timetables. These are obtainable from their local sites, from Tourist Information Centres, or by writing or phoning to the operators. Addresses, phone numbers and Internet addresses for these are at the end of this section.

The most comprehensive overview is *Getting Around Cumbria and the Lake District*, produced by Cumbria Connects: contact Public Transport Team, Cumbria County Council, Citadel Chambers, Carlisle, Cumbria, CA3 8SG or call 01228 606 000.

Stagecoach Cumberland produce *Lakeland Explorer* in a magazine-like format free, but not rucksack-friendly. It has details on relevant bus services and on lake steamers but not train timetables. Copies can be picked up on many buses.

## By Phone

Pti 2000 is a new national initiative to provide comprehensive telephone information, though there have been teething troubles.

*The Cumbria call centre is on 0870 6082608.

*National Rail Enquiries: 0345 48 49 50.

*TBC Hotline for main bus coach and rail routes throughout Britain: 0891 910 910.

## On The Internet

*Cumbria Journey Planner is the site for travel within Cumbria: go to http://www.cumbria.gov.uk/ and click on Journey Planner.

*For national travel UKPTI - The U.K. Public Transportation Site http://www.pti.org.uk/ describes itself, with some justification, as THE definitive index to timetables, fares, ticket-types, passenger facilities and lots more.'

*TheTrainline www.virgintrainsfares.co.uk is the on-line rail booking service. The array of different ticket types is confusing, but usually you can just click 'any'. Booking online earns a discount.

*Total Journey; http://www.totaljourney.com has replaced the Railtrack site. It gives up-to-date timetable information but seems slow to navigate.

*Useful, and with a campaigning slant is CountryGoer, http://www.countrygoer.org/ a national campaign to promote access to and within Britain's countryside by public transport.

## Transport Operators

*Virgin Trains*. Services on the West Coast Main Line (London-Glasgow), with stops at Lancaster, Oxenholme, Penrith and Carlisle. Advance booking is recommended. Many trains run close to capacity, and cheaper fares are only available if you book some time ahead. Telephone enquiries/bookings on 08457 222333. Internet enquiries/bookings on www.virgin.com or www.virgintrainsfares.co.uk

*Long-distance bus travel is by National Express Coaches: 0990 808080 or http://www.GoByCoach.com

*Stagecoach Cumberland* is responsible for nearly all bus services within the region. Phone enquiries now go to Pti 2000 on 0870 6082608. Advance booking is not necessary.

*First North Western* Trains runs local train services (Lakes Line, Furness Line, Cumbrian Coast Line). General enquiries go to National Rail Enquiries, 0345 48 49 50, while bookings can be made on 0870 60 66 007. However, advance booking is hardly ever necessary on these services. http://www.firstnorthwestern.co.uk/ is a

# Cumbria's Main Bus and Rail Routes

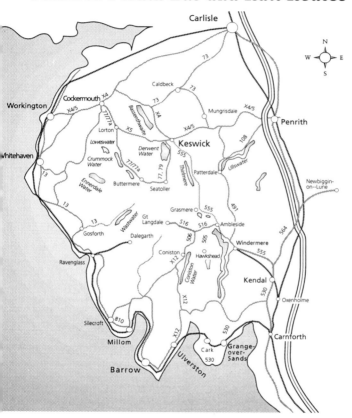

## Key

| | |
|---|---|
| ～～555～～ | road with bus route |
| ━━━━━ | motorway |
| •••••○••••• | railway/ station |

## Other Books by John Gillham and Grey Stone Books

**Car-Free Cumbria Vol 2: South by Jon Sparks**
The companion volume giving 14 linear day-walks plus a multi-day skyline walk between Silecroft and
Ambleside.

Paperback £5.95          ISBN 0-9540190-1-6

The following are on the Grey Stone Books Imprint

**Famous Highland Drove Walk by Irvine Butterfield**
Irvine Butterfield, author of the best-selling High Mountains of Britain and Ireland takes his readers in
the hoofprints of the last cattle drove in 1981, where 29 bullocks and a cow called Mathilda recreated
a journey across the Highlands of Scotland, from the Isle of Skye to the mart at Crieff in Perthshire.
In this 128-page book, he interweaves the story with background history and legend and offers walkers alternative high and low  routes, enabling them to plan this romantic journey across seven great
mountain ranges, Illustrated with both colour and black and white photos.

Paperback £9.95          ISBN 09515996-5-8

**Across Scotland on Foot by Ronald Turnbull**
Highly acclaimed by the press, this book gives its readers six inspirational coast-to-coast routes
across Scotland, plus ideas and practical advice for planning their own. An ideal present for both runners and walkers. 160p 210-148mm          Paperback £5.95          ISBN 09515996-4-X

**Peaks of the Yorkshire Dales by John Gillham & Phil Iddon**
A popular 128-page book which describes 31 mainly circular walks to the highest peaks in the
Yorkshire Dales.The celebrated mountains of Ingleborough and Pen-y-Ghent are featured alongside
lesser-known summits such as Great Coum above Dent and Rye Loaf Hill above Settle. There are 18
full-page colour photos and the maps are 3D panoramas.

Paperback £6.95          ISBN 09515996-1-5

**Long Days in Lakeland by Ronald Turnbull**
A beautiful coffee-table book that was highly acclaimed by the press. Illustrated with both black and
white and colour photos it takes the reader on ten epic Lakeland journeys, including 90-mile high
level crossing from Garsdale to the sea and a 95-mile tour of the major lakes, which is reduced to a
82 miles if you take the steamers. There's also a ten tarns tour and a Scafell Scramble circuit. For
those with less time on their hands, the book also includes ten daywalks and musings on the likes of
Borrowdale rain and Ullswater mist.

Hardback £17.95          ISBN 09515996-7-4

**Welsh Three Thousand Foot Challenges by Roy Clayton and Ronald Turnbull**
This 128-page book is based around the 27-mile Welsh Threethousands route. While Clayton guides
the walkers, Turnbull, an experienced fellrunner, gives the necessary advice for runners and walkers
who wish to pick up their pace. The book includes schedules by record holder Colin Donnelly and
former record holder, Joss Naylor as well as detailed advice on diet and injuries.
    Turnbull also describes in detail the 47-top Paddy Buckley round, which can be done as a
one-day run (for the elite) or a 4-day backpack and the story of near 200-mile Dragon's Back race.

Paperback £5.95          ISBN 09515996-6-6

**Lakeland Mountain Challenges by Ronald Turnbull and Roy Clayton**
This 160-page book is based around the 45-mile Lakeland Threethousands route. As in the Welsh
Three Thousands book Clayton guides the walkers, while Turnbull, an experienced fellrunner, gives
the necessary advice for runners and walkers . The book includes the Old County Tops, the Bob
Graham Round, the Four and More and the big horseshoe walks of the county.

Paperback £6.95          ISBN 09515996-8-2